THE
CORPORATE
DOMINATRIX

THE
CORPORATE
DOMINATRIX
SIX ROLES TO PLAY TO GET YOUR WAY AT WORK

LISA ROBYN

SSE

SIMON SPOTLIGHT ENTERTAINMENT
New York   London   Toronto   Sydney

Certain names and identifying characteristics of individuals mentioned in this book have been changed.

SꟾSꟾE

SIMON SPOTLIGHT ENTERTAINMENT
An imprint of Simon & Schuster
1230 Avenue of the Americas, New York, New York 10020
Copyright © 2007 by Lisa Robyn
Illustrations by Michael Nagin
SIMON SPOTLIGHT ENTERTAINMENT and related logo are trademarks of Simon & Schuster, Inc.
Designed by Jane Archer
Manufactured in the United States of America
First Edition   10   9   8   7   6   5   4   3   2   1
Library of Congress Cataloging-in-Publication Data
Robyn, Lisa.
The corporate dominatrix : six roles to play to get your way at work /
by Lisa Robyn.—1st ed.
p.   cm.
ISBN-13: 978-1-4169-4074-6
ISBN-10: 1-4169-4074-X
1. Women executives. 2. Dominance (Psychology). 3. Persuasion (Psychology).
4. Role playing. 5. Management—Psychological aspects.
I. Title.
HD6054.3.R63 2007
658.4'09082—dc22
2006031882

For Matt—
my husband, my best friend, my heart.

For my parents, Marvin and Gloria,
who taught me a thing or two about discipline.

In loving memory of Roslyn Greenberg.

Power can be taken, but not given.
The process of the taking is empowerment in itself.

—Gloria Steinem

CONTENTS

Foreword by M. Louise Ripley   xi

Introduction   1

CHAPTER ONE: MY BIG FAT SADOMASOCHISTIC WORK LIFE   7

- Freud for Thought   8
- Enter the Corporate Dominatrix   11
- The S&M of the S&P   13
- Power Becomes You   15
- Leather and Latex Research   16
- What Color Is Your Corporate Personality?   18

CHAPTER TWO: THE SIX SISTERS YOU NEVER KNEW YOU HAD   23

- Who Are You, *Really*?   24
- What's Your Dominance Quotient?   32
- The Many Faces of Power   36

CHAPTER THREE: ARCHETYPE ONE: THE GODDESS   39

- What's Your Earth Mother Mind-set?   39
- Get in a Goddess State of Mind with Personal Power   41

- Discipline #1: The Goddess Is Inner Directed   43
- Rule #1: Face-off with Your Alter Ego   46
- Discipline #2: The Goddess Has an Altruistic Nature   47
- Rule #2: No Go on Quid Pro Quo   49
- Discipline #3: The Goddess Is Centered at All Times   50
- Rule #3: Practice Creative Distancing   54
- The Dark Side of the Goddess   57

CHAPTER FOUR: ARCHETYPE TWO: THE QUEEN   59

- What's Your Matriarchal Mind-set?   59
- Get in a Queen State of Mind with Position Power   60
- Discipline #1: The Queen Rules with a Velvet Glove Instead of an Iron Fist   62
- Rule #1: Mediate, Don't Dictate!   67
- Discipline #2: The Queen Is Part Politician and Part Actress   69
- Rule #2: Image and Attitude Awareness Are Key   75
- Discipline #3: The Queen Is an Empire Builder   79
- Rule #3: Keep Your Cards Close to Your Chest   82
- The Dark Side of the Queen   83

CHAPTER FIVE: ARCHETYPE THREE: THE GOVERNESS   85

- What's Your Supervisory Mind-set?   85
- Get in a Governess State of Mind with Expert and Reward Powers   87
- Discipline #1: The Governess Is a Multitask Mistress   88
- Rule #1: Become an Organizational Whiz   95
- Discipline #2: The Governess Is a Natural Mentor   96
- Rule #2: Take Someone Under Your Wing   99

- Discipline #3: The Governess Builds Character and Follows Corporate Etiquette — 100
- Rule #3: Reach Out and Touch Someone — 106
- The Dark Side of the Governess — 107

CHAPTER SIX: ARCHETYPE FOUR: THE AMAZON — 109

- What's Your Mercenary Mind-set? — 109
- Get in an Amazon State of Mind with Coercive Power — 111
- Discipline #1: The Amazon Is Not Deterred by Defeat — 113
- Rule #1: Practice Healthy Fearlessness — 119
- Discipline #2: The Amazon Is Battle Ready — 123
- Rule #2: Make Skill and Preparation Your Weapons of Choice — 127
- Discipline #3: The Amazon Resettles Prisoners of War — 129
- Rule #3: Win the Peace, Not Just the War — 132
- The Dark Side of the Amazon — 133

CHAPTER SEVEN: ARCHETYPE FIVE: THE NURSE — 135

- What's Your Therapeutic Mind-set? — 135
- Get in a Nurse State of Mind with Healing Power — 136
- Discipline #1: The Nurse Has Steady Hands — 138
- Rule #1: Be Reactive, Not Radioactive — 139
- Discipline #2: The Nurse Takes Everybody's Temperature — 141
- Rule #2: Time for the Performance Checkup — 144
- Discipline #3: The Nurse Applies First Aid as Needed — 145
- Rule #3: Take an Aspirin and Call Me in the Morning — 150
- The Dark Side of the Nurse — 152

CHAPTER EIGHT: ARCHETYPE SIX: THE SCHOOLGIRL   153

- What's Your Scholastic Mind-set?   153
- Get in a Schoolgirl State of Mind with Borrowed Power   155
- Discipline #1: The Schoolgirl Tops from the Bottom
  and Bottoms from the Top   158
- Rule #1: It's Not a Bother, It's a Barter   160
- Discipline #2: The Schoolgirl Disarms with Charm   161
- Rule #2: Tap Into Your Inner Child   165
- Discipline #3: The Schoolgirl Flatters Through Imitation   167
- Rule #3: Audition for the Understudy   173
- The Dark Side of the Schoolgirl   174

CHAPTER NINE: THE CORPORATE DOMINATRIX GOES TO WORK
(AND WORKS IT)   175

- Playing the Hand You're Dealt   177
- The Corporate Theater of the Absurd   178
- Stage #1: Establish Your Defining Role   178
- Stage #2: Role Taking—Choosing the Part You
  Want to Play   180
- Stage #3: Role-playing—Lights, Camera, Action   182
- Role Reversal—Dominance Versus Submission   184
- Corporate Mind Games, Administrative Fetishes,
  and Exec-tricities   190
- The Corporate Dominatrix Self-assessment   194
- Play It Safe   196
- Fantasy Realization   199
- Manifest Your Destiny   200

ACKNOWLEDGMENTS   205

FOREWORD

This is the book I wish I could have read when I worked in the sado-masochistic field of corporate finance. This is the book I would like to have used when I first taught "Gender Issues in Management" at York University. This is the book I wish I had written!

There are numerous books available about women in management, women at work, women battling discrimination and harassment; books of case studies that outline scenarios in which working women find themselves; books that lay out laws and theories governing how things ought to function for working women; books on how women are socialized into the behaviors they exhibit in the workplace. But when as a professor of both business and women's studies I sought a book with which to teach the new course I had introduced, I could find no books out there that told about women's roles in management as I saw them, from the perspective of my own personal experience and that of so many other women I knew.

At first I thought perhaps my insistence that there was a sado-masochistic tinge to the whole thing came from my diabolically negative experiences in the corporate world colored by my own research into the realm of S&M for a book about surviving the particular cruelties of academic life. But in turning the pages of Ms. Robyn's *The Corporate Dominatrix,* I found validation for a view of the corporate world that had remained with me through decades, and for a view of how women ought to be fighting for their place in that world in which I had long believed.

In contemplating women's failure to move up the corporate ladder as quickly as men, for too long we have centered our focus on certain academic fields of study. We have examined the socializing effects of family, schools, the media, and advertising. We have studied the dissimilar ways that boys and girls are reared, counting, for example, on increased funding for girls' team sports to make a difference for the next generation. These factors are relevant, but they do not get at the heart of what needs to be recognized: The corporate world is a boundless arena in which power struggles are fought and won daily, and the sooner women learn how to wield power to their advantage, the sooner they will increase their chances for survival and success. In Ms. Robyn's own words, "Cultural conditioning can only be blamed for so long: Women executives need to take conscious control to break free of the bonds they perceive are holding them back. They can do this through understanding the different faces of power, and the six roles that carry that power."

Using the imagery of the six different roles played by the Corporate Dominatrix—the Woman in Control who can be alternately and sometimes simultaneously Goddess, Queen, Governess, Amazon, Nurse, or Schoolgirl—Ms. Robyn presents a delightful, easy-to-read text that takes us step-by-step through each kind of power, and how and when to use it. She provides examples of real-life women in specific work situations and tells us how they handled their individual problems, playing one or more of the six Mistress roles, wielding one or more of the different kinds of power. The book also has lots of easily read charts of comparisons so the reader can judge clearly the differences between approaches, and is full of useful quizzes to measure one's own standing in various categories.

Ms. Robyn has coined some gratifying phrases; among my favorites: "corporate vampirism," for management styles that suck away your energy and confidence, and "when someone tries to rattle your cage, remember you don't reside in one." This book should be required reading for every woman in management. My inner Dominatrix says, "Read it! Now!"

M. Louise Ripley, MBA, PhD
Associate Professor of Marketing,
Women's Studies, and Environmental Studies
Atkinson Faculty of Liberal and Professional Studies
York University
Toronto, Ontario, Canada

INTRODUCTION

I came up with the idea to do a women's business book with a sado-masochistic slant after a conversation I had with my boss several years ago. He told me my work life would improve dramatically if I acknowledged that business revolves around the concept of surrender. A red flag went up—I might be a tad too dominant for his taste, perhaps? As he explained his point of view (that I should be more submissive to authority), I wondered if he passed that advice along to the guys or if he was saving it just for us gals. In any case, the comment made me curious: to whom exactly was I supposed to be surrendering? And more important, how could I become the one who makes people surrender?

Coincidentally, a week or two later, I was surprised when a colleague referred to me as a "dominatrix," or "directress with a whip." A dominatrix, huh? It seemed like a left-handed compliment. So I Googled the term and discovered that the stock in trade of the professional dominatrix is role-play—balancing the power between submission and dominance, which is the essence of S&M. The two extremes stuck with me.

I was told to surrender, but I was perceived as a dominatrix, an interesting paradox. These types of behavior—domination and submission—seemed to be married in the workplace, and the more I researched the sadomasochistic lifestyle, the more I realized that there were parallels between S&M and corporate culture that offered insight into these inequities of power. A central credo of responsible S&M practitioners is "safe, sane, and consensual" (no one is made to do anything they're uncomfortable with or that is harmful in any way), and that's where the similarities between the two environments stopped—the workplace is often unsafe, sometimes insane, and rarely consensual. Even so, my discoveries deepened my understanding of the submissive and dominant forces at work and how I interacted with my colleagues. As I began to identify my supervisors, peers, and friends as submissives (or masochists) and dominants (or sadists), I translated my observations into rules that women can use to survive—and thrive—in the corporate world. Gradually friends, colleagues, and acquaintances in middle- and higher-level management positions began asking for job advice. My solutions helped advance their career objectives, and soon their professional self-worth soared.

Like many women who want to climb the corporate ladder, I've also had plenty of experience in sadomasochistic dynamics since entering the workforce. I've discovered that I am, in fact, a recovering masochist. Although my masochistic tendencies have abated, it began once upon a time, as it does for so many, with my earliest job experiences.

As a teenager I worked in retail clothing stores to get deep discounts on the latest fashions. The owners of the stores were tyrants, or, as I would call them today, sadists. I learned to keep my head down, rack up as many sales as possible, and develop relationships with customers so they would come back and ask for me. This approach, unlike that of the other staffers who slacked off, goofed around, or just didn't show up, was what eventually won over my bosses. I didn't identify it at the time, but I instinctively adopted the role of the Schoolgirl, which we will talk about in Chapter Eight.

Through college, I worked in the garment district in New York City to make extra money. Talk about an industry rife with perversity! Explosive personalities were rampant, and there were no boundaries between employer and employee. It was an anything-goes atmosphere of oversexed sales reps, flirtatious buyers, primadonna designers, and sleazy manufacturers. As a communications major, I found watching these interpersonal dramas fascinating. I developed a thicker skin and unwittingly assumed the role of the Amazon to survive, which we'll discuss in Chapter Six.

After work or classes I would hang out at CBGB or Max's Kansas City. It was the height of punk rock; the Sex Pistols, Blondie, and the Ramones were all the rage, as were mohawks, body piercings, and lots of leather. My friends took me on trips to retail sex-toy emporiums, such as the Pink Pussycat Boutique and the Pleasure Chest, and for some reason, I usually gravitated to the glass cases containing collars, riding crops, and whips.

When I asked the proprietors what kind of customers bought this stuff, they told me it was usually the types you'd least suspect: businesspeople, doctors, lawyers, and yuppie couples! I loved the fetish fashions (corsets, chain-mail vests, vinyl skirts, leather chaps, fishnets) so much that I went to a Halloween party as a dominatrix. I had a very superficial awareness of what dominas (professional dominatrices) did at the time, but I did feel very at ease in black leather. Perhaps it foreshadowed things to come.

As you can see, my fascination with S&M developed—however unconsciously—through my undergraduate escapades. I went on to get my master's degree in communications after completing my thesis on religious cults, and began applying that knowledge to the cult of management. There are certain similarities in the group thought processes, peer pressures, and insulated cultures that I noticed when I started out as a publicity assistant in book publishing. I was committed to being an invaluable asset to my boss, the associate publicty director. Everyone found this woman to be difficult, mercurial, and bitchy, but I knew I could learn a lot from her, so I ignored her quirks. I made it my mission to be the best at my job, and my commitment and determination paid off. I earned my boss's respect and trust, and was rewarded with the best mentoring that money can't buy. Of course, it got a bit strange at times when she followed me into the bathroom to ask me questions, or when she called my doctor to ask about a missing file while I was getting an X-ray, but I still gathered the necessary skills. Again the role of the Schoolgirl came in handy.

I learned that experience is your currency as you work your way up the management food chain. I was actively involved in every detail of the major PR campaigns she worked on, including books by Bette Midler and Martha Stewart. Since I was her right hand (and sometimes her left), it was a seamless transition to step in when she had an accident that required extensive surgery. Needless to say, my boss was very appreciative when she came back to work, and she never forgot how I held her office together while she recuperated. A nice promotion and raise soon followed, though I became keenly aware of the no pain, no gain connection in corporate life.

Fast forward to the present day—after holding executive positions in public relations, marketing, and editorial at major publishing houses, as well as running my own successful marketing communications firm, I've funneled my background and what I've learned from my S&M research into the magic of *The Corporate Dominatrix*. This book examines office behavior as a sociopolitical, neurotic phenomenon, and provides business-minded women—whether they are manager wannabes, middle managers, small-business owners, independent contractors, or entrepreneurs—with a set of rules to role-play by. Regardless of your age or generation, whether you're a Baby Boomer, Gen-Xer, or Millennial, you'll find the skills of the Corporate Dominatrix useful in any business interaction. *The Corporate Dominatrix* can give women the tools they need to move on and move up in their careers.

Just as professional dominatrices are in the business of helping others live out their fantasies, I'm in the business of giving women the strategies to help them achieve their dream career. *The Corporate Dominatrix* seeks to empower women and help them observe and understand the dynamics that impact their lives at the office each and every day—and become damn good at using them to their advantage.

CHAPTER ONE

MY BIG FAT SADOMASOCHISTIC WORK LIFE

My boss makes me feel like I'm an inch tall all the time! Part of me wonders if she secretly enjoys it. I try so hard to do everything right, and she still makes me feel incompetent.

—Tamara, tax attorney

I have a coworker who plays the victim; he thinks everything everyone else does is a personal assault on him. It's hard to get him to look objectively at his actions, or his contribution to projects, because his ego is so sensitive. I end up placating him and doing all the work.

—Jennifer, financial consultant

My supervisor needs a mother, rather than a strong number two person. It's like he wants me to take care of him all the time and treat him like a baby!

—Tamlyn, radio producer

My field doesn't seem to have a lot of women [in it]. *I have to be aggressive to keep up with the men, and sometimes when I do exactly what a male colleague might do in a tough negotiation, they treat me like I'm some type of crazy woman, or call me a bitch.* —Lucy, engineer

Do any of these situations sound familiar? Before we begin exploring how to master them, let's check out the origins of S&M.

FREUD FOR THOUGHT

Sadism is all right in its place, but it should be directed to proper ends.
—Sigmund Freud

Some background: Sigmund Freud, the father of psychoanalysis, borrowed the word "sadomasochism" from Richard Von Krafft-Ebing's classic work, *Psychopathia Sexualis*, which was published in 1898. Krafft-Ebing, interestingly enough, was affected by the writings of two European novelists, the Marquis de Sade, who wrote the infamous *Justine, or the Misfortunes of Virtue* and *The Hundred and Twenty Days of Sodom and Other Writings*, and Leopold von Sacher-Mascoh, who wrote *Venus in Furs*. Sacher-Moscoh, in particular, is worthy of note, since his story revolves around the protagonist's obsession with serving a dominant woman. Keep in mind that although aspects of S&M are fashionable in pop culture, it has deep historical and psychological roots.

8

What I'm asking is for you to see the darker edges of the workplace more clearly, instead of sugarcoating the truth or blindly accepting that it's part of doing business. I've read extensively about sadomasochism—*SM 101: A Realistic Introduction*, *The Topping Book: Or, Getting Good at Being Bad*, *The Mistress Manual: The Good Girl's Guide to Female Domination*, *The Master Manual: A Handbook of Erotic Dominance*, *The Loving Dominant*—and discovered the sadomasochistic power exchange that exists in an S&M relationship is eerily similar to the employer/employee power exchange in Corporate America. The push-and-pull, give-and-take, back-and-forth, ebb-and-flow rhythm is undeniable.

Have you ever offered an idea with passion in a meeting, only to be dismissed as being too "emotional"? Have you ever been mortified in a public forum? Treated like a child when presenting a project? Felt like a widget instead of a human being? Played mommy with your boss?

If you answered yes to any of these questions, then humiliation, infantilism, and objectification are not foreign behaviors to you—they are all common S&M techniques. Not surprisingly these dynamics are witnessed daily in the workplace. A situation in which some people have power and some people do not can lead to abuses by the people with power, and forcing those with less power to play a subservient role. Sadistic and masochistic personality traits are used in corporate life in an emotional and social, rather than sexual, sense (power relations, not sexual relations). Not only can corporate culture be dysfunctional, so is our perverse fascination with this power paradigm. In other words, we accept it, and play into it, and sometimes "get off" on it.

Add to this the forces that are reshaping the world of business today: rightsizing and downsizing, inflation and recession, mergers and acquisitions. The psychological uncertainty produced by today's brand of fluctuating capitalism and globalization causes anxiety, fear, stress, paranoia, and helplessness—dare I say, a sadomasochistic workplace of supervisor sadists and subordinate masochists.

A snapshot of Corporate America resembles some kind of de Sadeian fantasy come to life in offices nationwide. Need I mention Enron or Worldcom? The command-and-control model is still alive and well, where submission to bureaucracy and authority has become business as usual. If the organizational structure is flattening out, it's happening at a glacial pace.

Working women are particularly vulnerable in this environment. Why are they at risk? Some have the mistaken notion that kudos, promotions, and raises will simply come from a job well done. Ellen Snee, the founder and current president of Fine Line Consulting, a firm dedicated to the advancement of female corporate leaders, says, "Most of the women we work with are extremely effective leaders, but they're often not good at drawing attention to their achievements."

Female executives sometimes don't feel comfortable tooting their own horn, or playing with power or office politics. "Power is more important to men," says Ogilvy & Mather's current chief executive officer, Shelly Lazarus. "Men like to issue orders. They like to feel powerful. I get no thrill out of being powerful." Ann Winblad, Silicon Valley's leading software venture capitalist, says, "'Power' is a very dangerous word." And Mattel's ex–chief executive officer Jill Barad says, "When you apply the word 'power' to a man, it means 'strong and bold'—very positive attributes. When you use it to describe a woman, it suggests 'bitchy, insensitive, hard.'" Although women have made significant strides in the workplace, most are still conflicted about how their corporate power is perceived or acknowledged. So here we are, strangers in a strange new landscape where women are stuck. A new archetype is needed.

ENTER THE CORPORATE DOMINATRIX

The Corporate Dominatrix uses the tools of the professional dominatrix to succeed in the workplace. She understands that the key to effectiveness is to know how and when to switch roles according to the situations she faces. She knows when to be dominant (i.e., strong) and when to be submissive (i.e., flexible). She knows how and when to pick her battles. She is confident enough to intuit what her clients or colleagues need and want, and to respond accordingly. The Corporate Dominatrix exercises her power and mastery in the workplace using disciplines relating to attitude as well as technique. Faith Whittlesey said it best: "Remember, Ginger had to do everything Fred did, except backward and in heels."

Clearly we cannot wait for men (or even some women for that matter) to change corporate culture. We must take matters into our own hands and instigate change. Why, after so many years, are women still stuck? A study on social-dominance orientation published in the *Colgate University Journal of the Sciences* offers some clues. Researchers found that dominant women are viewed more negatively than dominant men, indicating that behavior inconsistent with gender roles is not well-received. The study also found that women who act according to their specific gender roles are viewed as more competent than women who do not. The trick to success is being able to succeed managerially while still remaining "womanly." As Duke University Basketball head coach and U.S. National head coach Mike Krzyzewski has said, "All leaders should embrace their inner woman." This leaves women with the quandary over which role to play; can they be both forceful and feminine?

If simple aggression were the key to the success of women, the office go-getters of the seventies, eighties, and nineties would have achieved total equality. Their no-nonsense approach would have catapulted them to the top, but that didn't happen exactly as planned. While this intense, take-no-prisoners style advanced those women's career trajectories, it only took them so far. This strategy often fails because gender roles in society have been clearly divided. For one thing, women traditionally have been more collaborative; many of them didn't feel comfortable in a more commanding role. If they could not compete by applying overwhelming force, they eventually dropped out or stopped climbing.

On the opposite end of the spectrum, the women who tried to cross the divide and overpower the competition were seen as bitchy and alienating. Obviously, being underwhelming does not work, nor does being completely overpowering. Women—even more so than men—must be dominating without being domineering. They can be seemingly submissive to management and acquiesce to authority at times—picking their shots without playing the victim—in order to get ahead. They must be able to play both roles. Think of it as being one part Laura Bush and one part Hillary Clinton. Women have to be firm and direct, but also compliant and flexible. They need to work harder at being included in informal networks. A woman who successfully melds these techniques—who can strategically assume the appropriate role for the situation—becomes the Corporate Dominatrix. And the Corporate Dominatrix always comes out on top.

THE S&M OF THE S&P

The Corporate Dominatrix examines the workplace for what it really is: a social sadomasochistic wonderland that must be approached with a new mind-set and a new methodology, working from the inside out, as well as the outside in. In case you're still thinking that sadomasochism, or S&M, is a frightening concept only practiced in an underground dungeon, think again. The concept has been a part of our daily lives for quite some time.

Consumers—yes, even savvy ones like you—have been bombarded, even seduced, by subliminal S&M messages over the decades. Popular culture reflects our fascination with S&M in fashion (Versace,

Dolce & Gabbana, Jean Paul Gaultier), body modification (piercings, tattooing), rock music (punk, goth, metal), and the photography of Helmut Newton. The popularity of movies such as *Secretary*, *Quills*, and *The Matrix* illustrates how S&M has tinged mainstream films, taking the sting out of the stigma.

Take common workplace terminology: "I'm on top of it," "This is going to get me to the top," or "It's lonely at the top." Conversely, we also say "I've hit rock-bottom" and "I'm stuck at the bottom." How about "I'm slaving away on this project" or "I've bottomed out"? Some S&Mers say that "top" and "bottom" are simply synonyms for "active" and "passive," respectively. I say absolutely! It's time we all saw the office for what it really is—a complex web of domination, submission, and corporate neurotica. As John Munder Ross notes in his book *The Sadomasochism of Everyday Life; Why We Hurt Ourselves and Others—and How to Stop*, "Nowhere in daily life is sadomasochism more constantly in evidence than in the institutions that constitute the workplace. It is here that the red threads of individual power and success are woven into a fabric of fixed and often labyrinthine bureaucracies whose function is to ensure institutional stability, viability, and with luck, profitability for all concerned."

In short, S&M in society has always been present under the surface; but it's only just started to come out of the dungeon.

POWER BECOMES YOU

Mastering others is strength. Mastering yourself is true power.
—Tao Te Ching

Power attracts, but it can also detract from your effectiveness, depending on how you use it. While sometimes it is absolutely imperative to fight for what you want, it can occasionally be just as wise to stand down or reassess your approach. Why force a power play when you can try diplomacy first?

There can be *power* in submitting to authority, as long as the submission is strategic. Every move you make is about advancement, and submission, in some cases, is the smart or only option available. When you are selectively confrontational, your boss and coworkers will see just how serious you truly are. You must flip the self-monitoring switch to see the importance of one issue over another. And sometimes it's smart to let people think you've surrendered. After all, it worked pretty well in the Trojan War. The power to evaluate, to determine priorities, to step up when necessary, and to role-play accordingly is what real control is about.

Most important, I use the phrase "power becomes you" because it does—power becomes part of you and your personality, for better or for worse. Inherently it makes you more magnetic and appealing. Understanding your own power and wielding it can add to your stature, state of mind, and certainly how others see you—and how you see yourself. As Margaret Thatcher once said, "Being powerful is like being a lady. If you have to tell people you are, you aren't."

LEATHER AND LATEX RESEARCH

According to Phillip Miller and Molly Devon, authors of *Screw the Roses, Send Me the Thorns: The Romance and Sexual Sorcery of Sadomasochism*, "Pro-domina[trice]s are in the business of fantasy realization and do not have sex with their clients. They are a cross between psychodramatist and therapist. A dominatrix, skilled enough to realize a living in the profession, earns every penny she makes. She must be confident enough to intuit and focus on the needs of many different personalities and strong enough to pull off scene after scene with expertise and finesse."

In order to put my S&M-workplace theory to the test, I did what any good investigative reporter would do, and scoured New York City for dungeons in order to speak with professional dominatrices about their experiences.

My research led me to Lady Kayla, the owner of Excalibur, an exclusive dungeon, a.k.a. house of domination. Lady K had been involved in the S&M scene, or community, for more than ten years and was interviewed as an expert in the HBO special *Fetishes: The Women of Pandora's Box*. Along with most of her fellow dominatrices, Lady K considers the fantasy realism of S&M sessions a form of erotic therapy. She makes no distinction between her highly orchestrated, masterful sessions and the services of a psychologist, social worker, or relationship counselor. She has a point—clients may even get more out of her sessions than they would ever get from conventional therapeutic treatment.

Twylo, a New York City dominatrix, muses: "If women stepped into the pumps of professional dominatrices, there would be a revolution! The things they would learn about other people's psychological makeup would amaze, confound, and ultimately enlighten them." Luckily for you, you don't have to—I did it for you.

Knowing when to be assertive and when to be acquiescent is the trick. Someone like Twylo, who is both a dominant and a submissive, is called a "switchable" in S&M speak. Some dominatrices can seamlessly go either way. They can turn on a dime. That's where the sense of theater comes in—of being an actress, of being able to role-play, of being in control of her dominatrix persona within whatever context or "scene" she is engaged.

This concept is inherent to sociodrama—simulating real-life situations to understand how people relate to one another. Socio-dramatists study the effect role reversal and role-playing has in solving problems and achieving goals. In short, you can't be on top all the time and you can't be on the bottom all the time. You want to become a switchable—that is the key to becoming the Corporate Dominatrix.

From Lady K, I learned that even the most successful men secretly want you to push back; they want to feel powerless for a change. I also discovered that it feels pretty damn good to be the one with total control.

Not a month later my newly conceived method of empowerment with an edge was put to the test when I had an altercation with someone at work. A male colleague had a habit of concealing problematic information only to eventually drop the bomb and have everyone else clean up his mess. But this time I chose to shame him into coming clean with all the details in a public meeting. The humiliation-and-embarrassment strategy worked. Not only did he apologize, he actually got down on his knees right in front of me to beg forgiveness! Okay, so I know he meant this as an amusing gesture, but *wow* . . . what a textbook slavish response to my challenge. I had really tapped into something.

WHAT COLOR IS
YOUR CORPORATE PERSONALITY?

How well do the S&M principles fit into our corporate schema? You'd be surprised. I'm sure you've had a sadistic boss or had to work with masochistic colleagues before, and chances are, you do now. As the former vice president of Marketing and Communications at a major publishing house, I've navigated and survived my share of corporate mergers, department shake-ups, political infighting, corporate misogynists, and office deadbeats. After years of participatory observation, I noticed certain trends about supervisors and their subordinates. Some of the best managers usually started out as exemplary, hardworking, devoted assistants who learned from good mentoring, while some of the worst managers usually began as devious, sycophant assistants who learned from tormentoring.

In other words, fascist bosses—those who take delight in

supremacy—create a sadistic management ethic and spread corporate vampirism, sucking the life out of employees. Democratic bosses, on the other hand, create a more even playing field and supportive work environment. Subordinates expect to be dominated to a certain degree. More interesting, though, supervisors often need—and secretly crave—to be challenged. Women seem to want to reconcile their authority and power in the workplace without sacrificing their femininity or individuality. A woman who can walk the line between hard business tactics and soft people skills breaks the office code and rises to the top. These realizations forever changed the way I manage and the way I *want* to be managed.

How do you want to be managed? Let's review your corporate makeup. Are you thick-skinned or do you bruise easily in your interactions at work? If the color of your corporate personality is black-and-blue, or just blue, you need to check yourself. How long have you been meaning to express a few concerns to your boss or colleagues? Do you share new ideas or ask for more senior executive responsibilities?

We all encounter stressful situations at work, and how we handle them affects not only our professional effectiveness, but our own well-being and sense of self-esteem. Corporate Dominatrix training will enhance your ability to be more successful on the job, using resilience and objectivity as your protective shield. Dominance training is based on the idea that by changing your roles and reactions (whether firm or flexible), you can change the dynamic of your relationships.

I've developed a chart to compare the striking differences among the Corporate Dominatrix, the Corporate Masochist, and the Corporate Sadist, so you can see for yourself the clear distinctions.

CORPORATE SADOMASOCHISTIC PERSONALITY TRAITS COMPARED WITH THE CORPORATE DOMINATRIX

CORPORATE DOMINATRIX

- Has clear boundaries; doesn't allow others to restrict or violate boundaries
- Conveys thoughts and opinions directly and clearly
- Expresses gratitude and appreciation graciously
- Uses direct eye contact, sturdy posture, assured gestures

CORPORATE MASOCHIST

- Allows boundaries to be ignored, violated, and regularly exploited
- Is inept at expressing thoughts and beliefs firmly and honestly
- Seeks validation and permission regularly
- Has shifty eye contact, sloppy posture, nervous gestures

CORPORATE SADIST

- Invades others' boundaries on a regular basis without remorse
- Expresses thoughts and actions in an overbearing, offensive way
- Belittles, marginalizes, and diminishes others
- Uses steely glares, finger wagging, fist pounding, aggressive mannerisms

For our purposes, here's how we will define dominance, submission, and sadistic behavior:

DOMINANCE is standing up for your rights in an open, honest, and direct way, which does not violate another person's rights (remember the S&M motto: safe, sane, and consensual). You have a responsibility to ask for what you want, make your feelings and opinions known, and act in a manner that is worthy of respect.

SUBMISSION is tactical compliance and appeasement; knowing when to back down or back off while keeping your rights intact. Express your feelings and concerns respectfully. Do not constantly submit to another person's needs or wants at your own expense.

SADISTIC BEHAVIOR is spewing feelings or stating directives in a manner that is demeaning, patronizing, discourteous, or offensive. The focus is exclusively on the outcome without considering anyone else's opinion or position. It may seduce you into thinking it's effective at first, but it ultimately spells disaster for yourself and others.

Regardless of the neurotic or dysfunctional behavior you run into at work as the Corporate Dominatrix, you will be able to analyze every situation, determine the best course of action, break down barriers, and move toward the best outcome possible.

Now you're ready to get up close and personal with the roles the Corporate Dominatrix uses to get what she wants when she wants it. Get ready to hang out with some ladies who are going to make your life a whole lot easier.

CHAPTER TWO
THE SIX SISTERS YOU NEVER KNEW YOU HAD

The Corporate Dominatrix can successfully apply role-playing models from her professional dominatrix cousin by using the six fantasy mistress archetypes: the Goddess (the spiritual you), the Queen (the sovereign), the Governess (the schoolteacher and mentor), the Amazon (the warrior), the Nurse (the caregiver and medic), and the Schoolgirl (the student and apprentice). Do any of these roles sound familiar? I'm sure you've unconsciously used some of them yourself. Now you will channel these heroines, consciously switching from one to the other to move up in your career. Remember, women are natural role players—we're mothers, sisters, daughters, girlfriends, wives, friends—so learning to apply the Corporate Dominatrix archetypes will be easier than you think.

WHO ARE YOU, <u>REALLY</u> ?

Below are some questions that will help you figure out which of these sisters are closest to your heart. After the questions, there are lists of defining characteristics that can help you determine which archetypes you naturally embody and where you want to focus your dominance training. If you find you don't relate to a particular type, don't sweat it—we'll work on that later in the book. Just acquaint yourself with the defining characteristics for now.

Ladies, meet your new siblings. . . .

DO YOU WORSHIP THE GODDESS WITHIN?

There are only two types of women—goddesses and doormats.
—Pablo Picasso

1. Do you listen to your own intuition instead of the office rumor mill?

2. Can you remain centered regardless of external forces?

3. Do you see the glass as half full instead of half empty?

4. Do you have a calming influence on those around you?

5. Is your inner world more important than the outer world?

If you answered yes to at least three out of five of these questions, you're levitating above the daily grind.

Defining characteristics of the Goddess

When in Goddess mode, you:

• maintain detachment
• look for meaning in your work
• see the good instead of the evil in coworkers and management
• choose the road less traveled
• take the higher ground
• don't sweat mistakes and confrontations
• work to achieve balance in work and life
• remain honest about your strengths and your weaknesses
• provide inspiration to others
• have a heightened state of awareness

DO YOU DEMAND THE RESPECT OF A QUEEN?

In every woman there is a Queen.
Speak to the Queen and the Queen will answer.
—Norwegian proverb

1. Do you like to be in a position of authority?
2. Do you have a tendency to be more involved in big ideas than details?

3. Are you energized by politics?

4. Do you consciously expand your domain to enhance your career and fulfill your vision?

5. Do you hold "court" in and out of the office?

If you answered yes to at least three out of five of these questions, you've got some royal blood in your veins.

Defining characteristics of the Queen

When in Queen mode, you:

- are royally assertive
- are goal oriented
- place a high emphasis on loyalty
- thrive on prestige
- enjoy privilege
- work toward building an empire
- delegate with clout
- network and make significant connections
- exercise benevolence and not malevolence

DO YOU KNOW HOW TO GIVE DIRECTION
LIKE A GOVERNESS?

Actions have consequences. Good behavior is rewarded.
Bad behavior comes with penalties.
—*Nanny 911*, the book

1. Do you enjoy the process of teaching and training?
2. Are you comfortable in a supervisory capacity?
3. Is organization your strong suit?
4. Do you remember the rules when others don't?
5. Do you like being entrusted with the management of others?

If you said yes to at least three out of five of these questions, you might have a flair for being a task mistress.

Defining characteristics of the Governess
When in Governess mode, you:
- display patience
- provide guidance
- have a strong sense of duty
- set up and maintain organizational systems
- are proactive
- are resourceful
- enjoy mentoring

- problem solve
- inspire cooperation
- are trustworthy
- don't contradict authority—you enforce it

ARE YOU A BATTLE-READY AMAZON?

As fierce as hell, or fiercer still, / A woman piqued who has her will.
—John Byrom, "Epistle to a Friend"

1. Are you conquest oriented?
2. Do you challenge people in authority if necessary?
3. Do you thrive on confrontation or conflict to restore order and justice?
4. Do you continue on another tack if defeated?
5. Are you a strategic thinker?

If you said yes to at least three out of five of these questions, you're a natural warrior.

Defining characteristics of the Amazon
When in Amazon mode, you are:
- independent
- heroic
- protective

- fearless
- industrious
- dynamic
- analytical
- courageous
- forceful
- decisive
- resolute

DO YOU APPLY FIRST AID LIKE A NURSE?

Panic plays no part in the training of a nurse.
—Elizabeth Kenny

1. Are you a healer at heart?
2. At work, do you feel like a paramedic for a corporate unit of *M*A*S*H*?
3. Are you sometimes better at taking care of other people than you are of yourself?
4. Can you determine when the atmosphere is reaching a boiling point in the office?
5. Do you have steady hands during emergencies?

If you answered yes to at least three out of five of these questions, put on your scrubs and grab your thermometer.

Defining characteristics of the Nurse

When in Nurse mode, you are:

• productively reactive
• a medicine woman
• responsive to emergencies
• composed
• humane
• respectful
• thorough
• fastidious
• observant
• a natural at administering remedies

DO YOU REMEMBER HOW IT FEELS TO BE A SCHOOLGIRL?

Flattery will get you everywhere.
—Mae West

1. Do you know how to play innocent to get ahead?
2. Can you appear nonthreatening in order to allow others to feel more knowledgeable than they really are, to stroke their egos?
3. Do you sometimes allow higher-ups to use your ideas as theirs to further your career?

4. Do you know how to use compliments in order to wrap coworkers around your finger?

5. Are you mindful of your place in the corporate hierarchy?

If you answered yes to at least three out of five of these questions, you're comfortable in your plaid skirt and Mary Janes.

Defining characteristics of the Schoolgirl

When in Schoolgirl mode, you are:

• the apprentice

• curious

• obedient

• interdependent

• acquiescent

• youthful

• playful

• respectful of authority

• coy

• lighthearted with a sense of humor

• mischievous

After looking these over, you may find that the role of Governess fits like a black leather glove while the thought of the Schoolgirl describes your coworker to a tee. You may be able to relate to some sisters more than others. By the time you're finished with this book, you'll be so familiar with all the archetypes, that you'll know *when* and *where* to use your Corporate Dominatrix skills for any situation that comes up—in work and in life.

WHAT'S YOUR DOMINANCE QUOTIENT?

Test it with the Corporate Dominatrix quiz. Let's see where you are on the dominance scale. Remember, honesty is the best policy. There are no wrong answers!

1. It's a month past your annual review, and you're still waiting to set up a meeting with your supervisor. You:
    a. remain in a holding pattern, since no news is probably good news.
    b. contact Human Resources to see if they can jump-start your boss into action.
    c. speak to your boss about arranging an immediate appointment to discuss your review and your retroactive raise.

2. The word at your company is that promotions are being held back for budgetary reasons. You:
    a. try to remain a company gal and ride out this bad patch.
    b. point out all the great work you're doing for further consideration when the freeze lifts.
    c. send your boss a memo outlining all your successes, and proceed with your promotion campaign undeterred, since rules are made to be broken.

3. Your supervisor always calls you in for a preparatory briefing before big meetings. Usually your best ideas become hers once you enter the conference room. This causes you to:

a. bitch and moan to all your colleagues.

b. plan to share only mediocre suggestions in advance.

c. tell your boss you'll present your ideas in the meeting.

4. An important client has a habit of making impromptu conference calls. Your immediate response is to:

a. drop everything and take the call.

b. talk for a few minutes, and then ask if you can call back.

c. refuse the call and schedule a mutually convenient time to speak later that day.

5. One of your direct reports is shamelessly playing up to your boss at your department's expense. You:

a. ignore it, since anyone can spot a kiss-ass.

b. explain to the employee that his behavior is bad for morale.

c. tell the employee to spend more time working and less time sucking up since his review is imminent.

6. Your company is poised for a radical reorganization. You:

a. feel assured when your boss says your job is safe.

b. start contacting executive recruiters for insurance.

c. ask your boss for a contract.

7. The director of another department is angling to take over your plum account. You decide to:

a. let it go so you're not as overwhelmed.

b. talk to your supervisor about it.

c. confront the director and tell her to back off your turf.

8. When senior executives interrupt you in meetings, you're most likely to:

    a. completely hold back your comments.

    b. wait till they've done talking, then finish your train of thought.

    c. ask that you not be cut off.

9. Your expense report from a company retreat gets returned with a question mark next to a massage. You:

    a. decide to pay for it yourself.

    b. point to other executives who charge massages to the company.

    c. get a doctor's note and resend to Accounts Payable.

10. The chief financial officer wants you to cut one hundred thousand dollars from your already diminished budget. You:

    a. do what you have to do.

    b. ask your boss to speak to the chief financial officer directly.

    c. appeal to the chief financial officer.

Corporate Dominatrix Matrix Scoring

Give yourself one point for every *a*, two points for every *b*, and three points for every *c*.

- If you got a score of 25 or more, you're highly dominant—an Amazon or a Queen.
- If you got a score between 15 to 25, you're moderately dominant—a Goddess, Governess, or Nurse.
- If you got a score between 15 or lower, you're imperceptibly dominant—a seemingly submissive Schoolgirl.

Highly dominant—You realize the importance of clout and a trusty riding crop. As a Queen or Amazon, you're inclined to stand up for yourself and not back away from confrontation. You rise to any challenge with zeal. But be careful, you need to be mindful of authority and not buck management too much. You may still need to develop a discerning mechanism to be a Corporate Dominatrix.

Moderately dominant—You want to have your cake and eat it, too. As the Goddess, Governess, or Nurse, you're trying to strike a balance between doing what's right for yourself, what's right for your company, and what's right for your colleagues. Balancing on a corporate tightrope can be exhilarating, but it can also make you dizzy. Your equilibrium is critical as a Corporate Dominatrix.

Imperceptibly dominant/seemingly submissive—You want to remain in the bosom of the rank and file. As the Schoolgirl, you're making sure you're still the teacher's pet, but that comes with dedication and hard work. Keep in mind that currying favor is okay once in a while, if it's opportunistic, but don't completely rely on it if you want to aspire to Corporate Dominatrix status.

*Note: If you're wondering how men fit in, there are three male types: Kings (highly dominant), Princes (moderately dominant), and Schoolboys (imperceptibly dominant and seemingly submissive). Male dominance and female dominance can coexist in the workplace by sharing power.

THE MANY FACES OF POWER

When you doubt your power, you give power to your doubt.
—Honoré de Balzac

The American Heritage Dictionary defines power as the ability or capacity to perform effectively. It is also the ability or official capacity to exercise control, authority, and forcefulness. Working women will go farther when they realize that power itself is not a bad or corruptive force. Like anything else, how it is used defines the way in which it is interpreted. Power can be becoming or unbecoming to the user. "For most women, power is a means to an end," says Kay Fittes. "This is a distinct contrast to the belief that men have. Men, more often, see power as the end. Power exists to have power. To embrace power, women must see what good is to come of it. Of all the differences between the sexes regarding power, this stance is the most profound of all."[1] Cultural conditioning can only be blamed for so long; women executives need to take conscious control to break free of the bonds they perceive are holding them back. They can do this through understanding the six mistress archetypes and the influence they exert.

There are different brands of power, just as there are different heights of high heels. The power that most people get stuck on is "position power"—the authority that management wields over their subordinates on an organizational chart. Most employees in

1. Kay Fittes, *Advantage* news 2, no. 6 (November/December 2005).

the corporate hierarchy get too fixated on rank, and don't realize they have other types of power at their disposal.

The Corporate Dominatrix understands how to use the "power dynamic" or "power trade"; this exchange allows an assistant to be dominant with a supervisor (topping from the bottom), just as a supervisor can be submissive with an assistant (bottoming from the top). Power is a two-way street.

Each one of the six sisters has her own signature type of strength, so remember: You are never defenseless as the Corporate Dominatrix. Here's the basic rundown:

THE GODDESS—Personal Power
THE QUEEN—Position Power
THE GOVERNESS—Expert Power (and Reward Power)
THE AMAZON—Coercive Power
THE NURSE—Healing Power
THE SCHOOLGIRL—Borrowed Power

Power is what power does, so let's define the types for more clarity:

Personal—Your character. The power that comes from feeling in control of yourself and your environment.

Position—Your status. Some measure of power is conferred on the bases of one's formal position in the organization.

Expert—Your knowledge. People who have the experience or expertise can wield tremendous power. It is possible, though, that an incredibly bright person can still feel powerless.

Reward—Your indispensability. People who are able to bestow benefits or perceived benefits hold power. Supervisors or coworkers with the ability to give promotions or even good internal and external public relations are valued.

Coercive—Your stick. This is your ability to use limited force when necessary. It may get results in the short term and be effective in combating unfairness or turf squabbles.

Healing—Your cures. The power used to foster a "healthy" work atmosphere and environment.

Borrowed—Your connections. Power through association; using someone else's power base on "loan" when you need it.

You always have a reserve of power, regardless of your title or level of corporate influence. The Corporate Dominatrix understands how to balance and properly utilize power, no matter what rank she holds or who she's dealing with. As you learn more about the six archetypes, you'll learn how to borrow power when you don't have it, or simply rely on your personal power if that's all you've got. Power comes from outside *and* within you, so take note and see if there is a specific type of power you seek more than others. And in time I'll show you how each archetype utilizes each kind of power.

When in Corporate Dominatrix mode, you will find the troublesome rival, controlling boss, and irksome colleague more easy to deal with and contain. You are moving toward a world where you'll be calling the shots, so well sometimes that others may not even know it. Let go of any clichéd, S&M preconceptions and open your mind. Become the mistress of your own destiny and career, and don't worry—this doesn't require using a whip . . . unless, of course, you want to!

CHAPTER THREE
ARCHETYPE ONE: THE GODDESS

WHAT'S YOUR EARTH MOTHER MIND-SET?

Before you work on communing with your inner deity, let's see how far you have to go to become a Goddess. Take a look at the statements below and rate yourself between 1 and 10. The higher you rate yourself for each statement below, the more accurate each statement describes your Goddess side. You . . .

1. work with integrity by staying true to your authentic self. _____

2. pursue inner-directed reflection over outer-directed aggression. _____

3. realize you are more than your job description. _____

4. usually take the higher ground. _____

5. play up the positive and play down the negative. _____

If most of your answers are below 6, you've been neglecting the Goddess within. This chapter will show you how to reconnect with her. If you're already in touch with your more spiritual side, this chapter might help you expand your horizons even more.

Everyone knows someone who displays her Goddess prowess more persuasively and comfortably than others, always with unflappable, zenlike calm. The most compelling trait of the Goddess is her inner calling to divine feminine powers. This woman is ethereal; she is not swayed easily by what others think, and she overcomes the mundane malaise of work squabbles, catfights, or problem projects. Essentially she values her private self and doesn't take anyone else's superficial impression of her too seriously. The Goddess seems to operate by a more profound set of rules and impulses. She finds meaning in her work and takes pride in her own decisions. She inspires the men and women around her, and she is a natural-born priestess, without always overtly preaching. When she is criticized or judged, she doesn't get defensive or paranoid—she takes in what is valid and takes the rest in stride.

GET IN A GODDESS STATE OF MIND
WITH PERSONAL POWER

Self-reverence, self-knowledge, self-control—
These three alone lead life to sovereign power.
—Lord Alfred Tennyson, "Œnone"

Self-possession and self-mastery are the essential traits of the Goddess. One of the most valued, specialized skills of the Goddess in the S&M world is that *she knows how to accept worship.* The mistress who acts out a Goddess fantasy thrives on reverential attention; slaves and submissives cater to her with praise, devotion, and adoration in the knowledge that she is inherently a deity. As Mistress Jacqueline in *Whips and Kisses: Parting the Leather Curtain* says, "Today I don't 'play out' my dominance. I am dominant. I don't 'make-believe' I am a Goddess. I am one."

The same goes for the Corporate Dominatrix Goddess in the workplace. Like the mistress fantasy, she knows her self-worth and inner strength. As the Goddess, you abide by a higher consciousness. You thrive on individual energy in all situations in business and in life, and regardless of your position or your responsibilities, you are strong on the inside. Even though others may mistakenly think you're under their jurisdiction, you are never anyone's servant but your own. Self-service is key.

The Corporate Dominatrix Goddess has a secure sense of self that keeps her in touch with her own sacred and unwavering strength.

You are to be adored because you are worthy and dynamic. If things go to hell at the office, your inner peace offers comfort and gives you poise. The Goddess operates with unshakable personal power, using individual energy that comes from within.

Even while playing other roles, whether dominant or submissive, you can come back to your Goddess energy when in need. There will be times, as a Corporate Dominatrix, when you must outwardly worship or cater to the demands of your job, a particular process, or senior management (idolatry, sacred cow syndrome). But inwardly—secretly—you should be worshiping yourself above all. Doing so will keep you from becoming too enmeshed in external circumstances.

Claudia Varrin, author of *The Art of Sensual Female Dominance* notes, "As a dominant woman, you will probably exhibit independent behavior that will exhilarate you and will be noticeable to those around you. The dominant woman does not engage in the codependent behavior that so many of her sisters seem to be mired in. By tapping into her own inner well of power, she finds her strengths and 'exploits' them herself. She doesn't walk around being apologetic for her personal power, but that doesn't mean she is rude or offensive. . . ."

Part of taking on the Goddess role is communing with your particular brand of divinity, your shamanic roots—not in a capricious, egotistical way, but in a kindhearted, charitable way. As you become better and better at this, the more you will find sustenance in it. All women have the light of the Goddess in them; they just have to know where to look. Once you find it, you will silence your most inarticulate, awkward, inadequate tendencies, and develop your self-knowledge, confidence, purposefulness, and awareness.

Start taking note of why you should worship yourself. What are your good qualities and accomplishments? Acknowledging your innate talents is what communing with your inner Goddess is about. Take a moment to write down your particular gifts.

Here is what one woman wrote:

"I make a great first impression."

"I'm a good, level-headed problem solver."

"I'm a lean, mean creative machine."

"I plan and execute kick-ass corporate events."

"I am gorgeous inside and out."

Discovering your Goddess can be as simple as reminding yourself of your achievements, both large and small—from welcoming a new assistant and introducing him around to receiving a prestigious award and sharing the limelight with your colleagues. It's all about the mind-set you *choose*, not the headspace something or someone puts you in.

DISCIPLINE #1:
THE GODDESS IS INNER DIRECTED

The Goddess is guided by her female intuition and taps into her genuine inner voice. We've all been in situations when we suffer from doubts and negative thoughts. It is normal but not productive. "I try to listen to that part of myself, deep down inside, that reassures me, I'm damn good at my job, when anything threatens my confidence," Kim, a market analyst, said.

Even women with healthy egos fall prey to destructive office or industry gossip. By using Corporate Dominatrix Self Talk, you can combat any Masochist Self Talk (or just plain negative office chatter). Take a moment to see where in the following examples you fit in:

MASOCHIST SELF TALK	CORPORATE DOMINATRIX SELF TALK
I'm too insecure to contribute to the meeting.	I was specifically invited to share my ideas.
I can't believe I made such a stupid mistake.	No one is perfect, and I can learn from the experience.
Loosing my temper is a sign of weakness.	Managing my emotions is a sign of strength.
I'm going nowhere in this job.	I'll volunteer for projects that are leading somewhere.
Everyone is so much more experienced than I am.	I can learn a lot from these people.

Learning how to decipher between your authentic voice and the doubting voice that drains your confidence is a Corporate Dominatrix discipline. When you have a million thoughts dancing in your head, focus on the ones that will give you clarity and strength, regardless of the climate that surrounds you—that is essential for the survival of a good Goddess.

Marcy, an engineer, had been slaving over a proposal for a year for a new city bridge, and was sure it would pan out. She'd pulled long hours rewriting and reworking the plans, and schmoozed all the players involved who would green-light the project. One day she discovered that even though she was promised funding, the board members of her company decided to switch gears and give the go-ahead to a coworker with a less expansive, less costly plan. "I was distraught and felt like the rug had been pulled out from under me. Was my proposal that bad? Was my idea that poorly designed?"

Suddenly, a swarm of different obsessive thoughts about how she wasn't worthy or how the board members might be out to get her began swirling in her head. She felt defeated by those masochistic, negative thoughts. When she turned to me for help, I walked her through the process of activating her Goddess, and she decided to revisit the decision the board made to squash her beloved project. She needed to let go of her ego, take the board's criticisms and concerns to heart, and accommodate them to get a second chance. After rethinking her plans and using Corporate Dominatrix Self Talk, she made a presentation to the board, showing that the project could be done within half the time allotted, therefore saving more money than she had initially requested. The board liked her passion for the project and unanimously agreed she could move forward. If she had gone in there without the Goddess, or the self talk, she might not have made out as well, and could still be stewing in her own self-conscious worries.

Hanna, a producer for a film production company, felt that her boss frequently discounted her opinions. We talked and I could tell right away—Hanna was not listening to her inner, authentic voice; she was listening to all of the doubts that were affecting her body language (which came off as tense) and her voice (more tentative than direct). When she finally got the hang of using the Corporate

Dominatrix Self Talk rather than the Masochistic Self Talk, her presentation (body, voice, and energy) changed for the better.

It takes thirty to sixty days to break a habit, so you'll need to keep trying the Corporate Dominatrix Self Talk until you succeed. Regardless of whether you're having a good day or a bad day, when masochistic thoughts fill your head, try to combat that negativity with some positive strength. Remind yourself of your aspirations and stay focused; listening to your authentic voice will keep you centered. As one very successful magazine executive, Emma, said, "I rely on my intuition in handling most matters. As I have aged, I have learned that trusting my instincts is often the wisest path to choose."

RULE #1:
FACE-OFF WITH YOUR ALTER EGO

Try using Corporate Dominatrix Self Talk when putting on your makeup or blow-drying your hair while looking in the mirror. Remember, talking to yourself is a sign of mental health! By listening to your authentic voice, you will drown out the other doubting thoughts. Look in the mirror and say out loud all the good things about yourself you need to be consciously aware of. When no one else is around, you can brag your heart out.

To focus on your Corporate Dominatrix Self Talk, these tips are helpful:

- Set goals for yourself.
- Be optimistic since pessimism saps your energy.
- Don't get distracted by outside noise; stay in the moment, even if it's not comfortable.
- Remind yourself how talented you are daily—self-ego-stroking is allowed!
- Post mantras or sayings that inspire you, and read them often so they stay top of mind.

This technique works particularly well before a challenging meeting, a performance review, or any situation where you need some additional Goddess oomph. Conversely, when you anticipate the bad stuff before it happens, you're putting some harmful energy into your environment. For example, if you go into a business meeting expecting negative feedback, your body language and verbal communication skills will give you away, and your audience might capitalize on your vulnerability.

DISCIPLINE #2:
THE GODDESS HAS AN ALTRUISTIC NATURE

The Goddess gives to others out of the goodness of her heart. She understands the essence of charity. Margaret, an associate director at a TV station, said, "When I give support to coworkers, even if it's not entirely necessary, I'm building a rapport with them. By giving, strangely enough, I become a stronger person. It adds to my character." Showing generosity to others at work and being considerate with your time or energy can boost your self-esteem.

There's something to be said for thinking about others. Is a colleague struggling with a project that you can help with? Gracie, a customer relations exec, said, "I try to help others. It builds a bond between my associates and me. Even if it's not in my department, I'm all ears when someone needs to clear the air or just brainstorm." In the long run, in Gracie's case, going the extra mile is going to engender a great reputation throughout the company.

Generosity is also needed in situations when you're being pulled to the darker side of your personality. Regardless of how much you might yearn to plot revenge on the vice president or to grab an intern by the collar and toss them out the door, when you consciously choose the Goddess, you will be more respectful and tolerant. In a sense, this role is of the Pollyanna/Goody Two shoes of the office. She always does the right thing, even if the she-devil inside her is trying to get out. For this reason, the Goddess can be one of the toughest, most challenging archetypes to slip into—it's hard to be thoughtful and patient and not lose your cool when you are frustrated or irritated.

We've all had punishment fantasies, but rather than acting on those impulses, the Goddess gets her way by disarming people with her big-heartedness. For example, the Goddess would be effective in these scenarios:

• One of your archrivals is trying to push your buttons so that you blow up in front of a customer and lose your cool. Instead keep your composure and throw him off guard by remaining professional and attentive to the customer, and indifferent to your competition.

- A coworker is spreading gossip that you're slacking off on a project to elevate his standing. Instead of getting paranoid and defensive, you calmly set the record straight and make sure you let the team know about your contribution.

The Goddess is gracious and takes the high road in tough situations, no matter what her inner temptation might be. She understands forgiveness and uses positive energy in order to resolve conflicts to her advantage. That includes the daily, petty instances, not just the major confrontations. It's the Goddess who goes out of the way to help an intern with the paper jam in the Xerox machine. Magnanimous gestures matter, especially when they accumulate to form a stronger Goddess within. What goes around comes around.

RULE #2:
NO GO ON QUID PRO QUO

Quid pro quo, Latin for "an equal exchange" or "I give so you give," is an attitude that the Goddess does not abide by; she doesn't necessarily expect payback. If she's unselfish, she understands that it may not result in a direct reward for her, at least not immediately. The Goddess does not participate in the "What's in it for me?" attitude.

Having an open door-policy and inspiring an atmosphere of trust, respect, and tolerance may not figure into the number of zeros in your salary, but they will help you build strength within yourself.

By offering your time and support with no strings attached, you'll rack up those karma points. (I promise they do matter!) And remember: The way to be worshipped—and to worship yourself—is to do something unselfish, even when you feel like looking out for number one. The Goddess's first priority is *not* her own agenda or self interests. She always does the right thing.

DOMMERCISE:

A great way to avoid thinking "what's in it for me" is to try devoting a few hours a week or month toward a charity. You'll feel terrific after you direct your time and energy toward something besides yourself. "I began donating a couple hours every other week to a Big Sister/Little Sister program for inner-city girls. It helped me adjust my perspective when I started taking things too seriously at work," Stephanie, a marketing assistant, said.

DISCIPLINE #3:
THE GODDESS IS CENTERED AT ALL TIMES

The Goddess uses her personal power to take inventory of what she does have instead of what she doesn't have. If you're constantly whining about something you don't have and not focusing on the present moment, you'll develop a reputation for being ineffectual. When you let your emotions control your actions and have public scenes where you fall apart, people take note and lower their estimation of you. Allowing yourself to go into a tizzy wastes time and energy, and in the end, you lose sight of the quickest, wisest way to make a situation work. Learning how to center yourself is learning how to see your job in the grand scheme of life.

"If I let myself start freaking out about things I can't control or things that have more to do with my ego and less with my self, I feel out of whack," one ad agent, Kathy, said. When emotions start coming on strong, you need to ask yourself what's really at stake? Centering yourself puts things into perspective.

The Goddess can help you refocus and realign your interests and peace of mind. Let's look at Sandy, a vice president at a large consumer products company in the midwest, who got an offer to move to their New York City headquarters. When she saw her office, she called me, horrified. "It's a closet," she shrieked. "There's no way I can work in that space, let alone have meetings there." She fully intended to rush into her boss's office in an angered frenzy.

After talking Sandy off the ledge, I asked her to first center herself and calm down. Then I asked what a larger office represented to her, and she said it signaled power and prestige, something that was highly prized in her business. The bottom line was, would the current office inhibit her from doing her job? The answer was no. So, Sandy was focusing on the external trappings of power to feed her ego. Since this was so important to her, we scripted a conversation she could have with her boss where the size of the office was grounded in good business sense, not superficial egocentricity. No anger or hysteria allowed—she must be fully centered to keep her professional cool.

I asked her to poll other executives in her industry to see how many of them had offices with a meeting area. That way she could make a solid case: I want to close deals and make money for the company, and I need every advantage possible in a competitive environment. Though her boss appreciated her point of view, there were no larger offices available, but they agreed to revisit the issue in the new year. In the meantime, he did find a conference room for Sandy to use for business meetings.

Instead of giving in to her disappointment, she needed to regroup, take inventory of what she did have instead of what she didn't, establish herself in her new situation, and prove herself—that would go a lot farther than throwing a temper tantrum in the first week of work. She had a new job, and she needed to focus on doing it well and not count ceiling tiles.

In truth more and more workers today don't even have an office, since they can stay connected through laptops, PDAs, cell phones, and taking meetings in other people's offices. You can conduct business from anywhere, and that has made deluxe offices with multiple assistants a thing of the past for all but the most senior executives.

The Goddess's talent for centering herself can help her refrain from temperamental explosions when she feels hurt, beaten down, or betrayed, and makes her refocus on what's really important. She's a veritable Houdini with the ability to escape corporate chains, such as public ridicule, back stabbing, bad performance reviews, or inefficient workers. Instead of becoming weighed down by the bondage of hierarchical bs, she is uplifted by objectivity and is true to herself. "When I become frustrated with something at work, little things can seem big, and make me lose track of what's really important—like my sanity!" one ad director for a telecommunications company, Danielle, said.

Here is a Goddess centering exercise that comes in handy when you need to return to your personal power:

1. To begin, get in a comfortable position, whether on a couch, chair, or in bed.
2. Focus your attention on the center of your chest or on your Third Eye (this is the eye that is spiritually present in the middle of your forehead).
3. Breathe in and out, with the inhalation shorter than the exhalation. On the exhalation, push the air and negativity out completely, and on the inhalation, breath in and allow positive energy to reenter the body.

While doing this mental workout, imagine upon exhalation that those masochistic thoughts and impulses are leaving your mind and body. Replace them upon inhalation with encouraging thoughts and inclinations. The Goddess's spiritual backbone is Kundalini energy (cosmic energy that activates the consciousness). She is in touch with an inner knowledge and vitality that is more powerful than bureaucracy's external forces.

During your centering exercise—whether you're at home or at work—remember the following Goddess-centering self-affirmations:

- *I will free myself from the opinions, attitudes, or feelings of others about me and feel good about myself.*
- *I take personal responsibility for my well-being.*
- *I will let go of emotional baggage.*
- *I will resolve feelings from the past so that I can face the future with confidence.*
- *I will achieve my fullest potential.*

Uncovering the Goddess can be invaluable to preserving your peace of mind and your ultimate goals. If you practice centering yourself regularly, you will discover better solutions to problems and get through tough or challenging situations with more savvy. Unflappability and a confidence in your value and worth will help you combat the abusive S&M forces in your job.

RULE #3:
PRACTICE CREATIVE DISTANCING

Compartmentalizing or separating yourself from negative or aggravating work situations or people is what creative distancing is all about. This Goddess method helps you retain your objectivity. If you escape the tangles of work ordeals, you will find it easier not to fall victim to harmful cycles that will allow your job, coworker, or boss to control your spiritual self. For example, Sandy worked on distancing herself instead of identifying her self-worth with the size of her office—she was able to look past it and began making a great first impression on her new boss and colleagues rather than acting out. It was easy to see the most productive way to handle some corporate challenges was to creatively distance herself.

Heather, a journalist, said, "If I don't get the promotion I want, I don't allow it to influence my personal outlook or self-worth. I try to gain some objectivity and remember, yes, I need to change my plan, but in the end, I've got to remember, it's only a job."

The strength you receive from creative distancing may not be overt, and your boss or coworkers may not be immediately aware of it, but it will help you overcome situations in which you feel inadequate or trapped. When you want to get away from the melodrama at work, remember this: *There is a higher power stronger than the corporate structure and it's in you.* In any bureaucratic situation, creative distancing can ground you before you lose your sense of self. The Goddess will bring you back from egocentric, damaging behavior. It is the ego that is easily bruised or hurt by off-handed comments or actions, and the Goddess must counter that by knowing that the offense has nothing to do with her true self-worth.

Creating a "buffer zone" is critical to your professional survival since you need to create boundaries between the professional you and the personal you.

"My husband always complains that I take work home with me, mentally and emotionally . . . and I guess it's true. It's just hard for me to get out of my work mode. When I lay down at night, I start to think of things I should do at work the next day," said Teresa, a schedule manager for an export company.

Whether you are a novice or a veteran executive, management can practice a unique type of corporate vampirism, and suck your energy and your confidence. Since we work in a 24/7 environment, it's hard to disconnect from the office due to e-mail and voice mail; the lines between our professional and personal lives have blurred. Where do your lives intersect?

Be honest—when you put boundaries around these three spheres, are they clear? Do you take calls after work, and allow them to disrupt dinnertime with your family? Do you have *you* time?

Where these circles intersect is where you need to create shock absorbers that separate your subjective experience from your objective experience. Let's call this new awareness, or creative distancing, a type of consciousness cushioning.

DOMMERCISE: Keep Those Bugaboos at Arm's Length

Here are some tips to help you practice:

- Don't take ownership of responsibilities and/or actions that don't belong to you. Graciously step aside and let others take their fair share.
- Be kind to yourself after mistakes or missteps, and learn from them. Nobody is perfect!
- Try hard not to personalize what isn't about you. Don't let your demons get the best of you.
- Form an external sounding board you trust, and listen to what they have to say.
- Take a deep breath and don't overreact. Modulate your response to fit the situation at hand.
- You don't have to buy what other people are selling.
- You are not your job. Develop outside interests and hobbies.
- When someone tries to get your dander up, remember, don't fall for the ploy.

THE DARK SIDE OF THE GODDESS

Beware of becoming too New Age: Don't let your soul sister have you chasing moonbeams. Make sure your feet are firmly planted on the ground and in reality. As one jewelry designer, Krista, said, "When things were going downhill at my job, I felt the universe was sending me a signal that it was time to fulfill my dream of opening my own online jewelry store. I hired a Web designer, made all the earrings, necklaces, and bracelets, and launched my website within a few weeks of quitting my old job." After three months of minor returns on her investment, Krista realized it may have been frustration and not the universe that influenced her decision. She needed to be more hard-nosed about a practical business plan, and less dependent on good karma.

DOMMERCISE: Take Some Time Off

When you want to find your inner Goddess, try taking a yoga or meditation class. Introduce feng shui into your office or home to increase the flow of energy and help you to become calmer.

Now that you've gotten the run down on how to rule your personal domain, the Queen can show you how to take care of your career empire.

CHAPTER FOUR
ARCHETYPE TWO: THE QUEEN

WHAT'S YOUR MATRIARCHAL MIND-SET?

Let's check to see if you are a member of the aristocracy. Take a look at the statements below and rate yourself between 1 and 10. The higher you rate yourself for each statement below, the stronger your noble presence. You . . .

1. like to call the shots rather than take orders. _____
2. are ambitious and look at the big picture. _____
3. network like there is no tomorrow; you know that status is more important than status quo. _____
4. wield power with confidence. _____
5. enjoy being the center of attention. _____

If most of your answers are below 6, you need to work on your royal presence. This chapter will show you how to strengthen your Queen. If you think you've got the hang of it, you may still have a thing or two to learn. . . . Read on!

Modern-day Queens—like Condeleezza Rice, Martha Stewart, and Oprah Winfrey—possess an air of nobility. The Queen flexes her aristocratic muscles, delegating tasks and responsibilities while keeping her eye on territorial goals. She assigns duties rather than hoarding them, and enjoys the power of privilege that comes with her position. With the larger objectives in mind, she avoids micromanaging small projects. She is a political animal and cultivates her empire through vision, negotiation, and mediation. Always surveying the landscape, this crowned diva knows how to expand her business or corporate realm.

GET IN A QUEEN STATE OF MIND WITH POSITION POWER

I will not be triumphed over.
—Cleopatra

By leveraging her authority, the Queen is able to rule with impunity. Position power is derived from the rank you hold in the context of a hierarchy; it is your position that allows you to bestow favor on those around you. Titles are sometimes important in position power; a smart Queen is always aware of where she is on the organizational chart. Management has legitimate power over you, and if you are a boss, you have the same kind of authority over the people that report to you. It is this power that can be used for guiding teams to success or driving them into the ground.

In the S&M scene, submissives pay tribute to and curry favor with the Queen, often by giving thoughtful gifts. I've talked to mistresses whose clients bring them things they think they'd enjoy, like flowers, perfume, or S&M accessories, such as an expensive cat-o'-nine-tails. If the gifts are not adequate or to their liking, they are exchanged or returned with the snap of a finger or slap of the wrist. These offerings, or tokens, of respect are meant to win points. Even so, this royal fantasy-mistress is not easily influenced. Pleasing her is just one of many hurdles to jump for the Queen.

The Queen role in the workplace is somewhat similar to her S&M counterpart. She understands how to use her power within the organization to make the command-and-control model work for her. Her colleagues may seek to win her attention, anticipating her needs to make sure her department, company, or office is profitable. The Queen doesn't get stressed about micro issues or the administrative details of her job. While her characteristics compliment managerial positions, use of the Queen role isn't limited to only higher-ups. You can also be the Queen among assistants or the Queen among coordinators. Wherever you are in the corporate structure, you can focus on goals without getting bogged down in petty details or allowing your long-term vision to get sidetracked by palace intrigue or mind-numbing chores.

DISCIPLINE #1:
THE QUEEN RULES WITH A VELVET GLOVE
INSTEAD OF AN IRON FIST

As a Queen, you need to understand the principles of democracy to avoid blatant narcissism or omnipotence. Are you a fair and just ruler? Are you avoiding the power-trip trap that many dictators fall into? A good Queen has a solid vision for her queendom's future, not just her own majesty. Whether it's an achievable profit margin, an upgrade in a technological system, or a reorganization of a department, she knows that if her employees do well, so does she. The Queen envisions everyone working together as a whole to achieve something for the collective good rather than becoming trapped in an insular, egotistical drive toward her own glory, greed, or lust for power. She rules with fairness and free enterprise.

As Carrie, a senior copywriter writer, said, "My boss is such a great supporter when I have ideas. She embraces my good suggestions (and gives me credit) rather than feeling threatened by them. Now I try to do the same thing with my assistants." Carrie understands that to strengthen her position, she has to encourage her direct reports.

Malevolence provokes mutiny, and benevolence wins loyalty. The Queen understands that a winning attitude toward her colleagues contributes to the cohesiveness of her team. She knows when to use negotiation instead of ultimatums. As one Queen,

Sheila, a media executive, said, "I try to treat my direct reports and coworkers as I would like to be treated—with respect."

DON'T JUST OFFER DECREES WITHOUT DISCOURSE

Lucy, head of a marketing consulting company, was technologically progressive and wanted all of her departments to begin sharing information. Employees were used to playing phone tag or e-mailing a dozen times a day to accomplish a single task. She saw that a new collaboration and document management tool would realize her vision for a cutting-edge company that ran more efficiently. "I want all of my employees to be on the cutting edge with advanced technological skills. If they are savvy with the latest and greatest software, my company will be ahead of the game."

There was grumbling throughout the departments. Everyone would have to take time out of their already busy schedules to learn a completely new system.

I advised Lucy not to issue decrees without supporting explanations. She needed to answer questions and process feedback. A Queen in a castle, on a hill, out of touch with her people is not going to be favored by the masses. She needed to make sure that her decision was perceived as a strategic one rather than a mandate from an authority figure who doesn't understand the concerns of her employees. To act the role of a nonpartisan Queen, she should openly explore the concerns of her employees and hold focus meetings while providing testimonials from other companies with the same application.

When she presented a fair and balanced representation of the system's advantages, everyone understood her reasoning was sound, and most supported it. As one employee said, "It was painful in the short term, but essential in the long term."

THE TOOLS TO RULE

Another class-A Queen, chief executive officer of the Home Depot Inc., Carol Tomé, similarly decided to aggressively upgrade the company's information technology, and saw increased returns. She has continued to make tracks by encouraging employees—especially women—in positive, supportive ways that lead them with diversity and vision to success. With currently only ten women as chief financial officers at Fortune 100s and only thirty-five in Fortune 500s, it's obvious Tomé had to be a great leader to get to the top. Her reign includes more than just outstanding accomplishments; her employees love her.

Her direct reports say she's given them "new tools and logic" to eventually get where she is.[2] Tomé stresses that women must support one another, and in doing so, she works on supporting her employees. She suggests that little things matter, even details such as grabbing a chair next to another woman at a meeting. She took the velvet glove to the next level and started what she calls the "Velvet Hammers," a group for women who need to leverage their leadership. These ladies spread the love in their mission to help other women—through networking, sponsoring speaking engagements for women, and donating to Girls Inc. (a nonprofit initiative to empower young women). Her employees say this is just one example of how Tomé leads and encourages productivity and positive results from her employees—through being inclusive and listening to them.

2. Susan Kelly, "Who Says Women Can't Work with Tools? Not Home Depot," *Treasury & Risk Management*, November 2005, http://www.treasuryandrisk.com/issues/2005_10/careers/473-1.html.

The method that Tomé and most good Queens embrace is what some call "participative leadership," whereby employees feel honored, respected, and therefore learn more by understanding why the Queen is doing what she is doing. Beginning new initiatives and allowing your employees to hear only through the grapevine, or steamrolling them into something without inviting them to participate or contribute on some level, will get you nowhere fast. For example, cutting back a department's expense account without telling them why you're doing it or asking for suggestions as to how to do it, is not using participatory leadership. Allow your subjects to feel appreciated through their involvement rather than uncomfortable when they contribute or speak up.

Judith, a sales executive at a manufacturing company, wanted to develop a business outside the typical consumer base. Rather than just giving orders and doling out tasks, she began by holding meetings with her department to share her vision and goals and to invite input. This way, her people would have a stake in the new venture and an improved understanding as to why they would be taking on more work than their typical accounts. By involving them, she got ideas from her direct reports she hadn't even considered, thus expanding her vision. Like Judith, many leaders have found that employees are more collaborative, cooperative, and less competitive when they are working on joint goals.

Even when your employees contribute, as the Queen you still direct your employees' efforts—you still have your position power. If you're afraid of losing a foothold, tell that control freak in your head to get a grip. Chances are, if you develop your own style of participatory leadership, or use your velvet hammer—you will gain a larger empire instead of being perceived as dictatorial. It's better to gain control through openhandedness rather than insecurity.

HONOR YOUR EMPIRE'S STRENGTHS

A Queen must always bolster and support diversity with her colleagues through communication; she will know what her queendom needs by encouraging a give-and-take of information. And if she fulfills those needs, that will, in turn, fuel her strength and favor with her people. As a Queen you should appreciate democracy in action. Avoid the temptation to see everything as one without taking note of individual strengths, weaknesses, or differences. Alexander the Great was a genius at acquiring new territories, but his empire was strong because he respected individual customs and beliefs and did not expect territories to accommodate one another. They were separate in their identities and strengths but united under his rule.

"I think the more talents and skills I bring to my department, the better. I don't want every single person to be a clone with the same background. For example, I had four men as my direct reports and saw the need for more women. Different perspectives help foster new ideas," said Carol, a sales executive for a national bookseller.

A Corporate Dominatrix Queen honors each employee and each department's skills, even if they are not the same as her own. If she is a marketing executive working with the editorial department, she will respect their talents and skills, and allow them to serve the overall good of the company rather than assume she knows how to do each of their jobs and treat them disrespectfully.

She welcomes diversity, individuality, ability, and originality; all these different elements can unite to complement the queendom.

RULE #1:
MEDIATE, DON'T DICTATE!

One good Queen, Evanne, a telecommunications executive, explained that she is straightforward with her direct reports rather than berating them when they make mistakes. "There is a difference between dictating and delegating; letting go of some tasks will help others become more skilled, experienced, and confident."

As a Queen you should avoid edicts or dictums, and instead:

• *Use your authority as a Queen to mediate and smooth the rough edges during department friction.* Laurie, an executive in a financial management company, had two direct reports who were seeking clients in the same areas, and tended to be at odds with each other. Their competitiveness was interfering with the tone in the office. "I sat them down and really picked their brains: Did they both really have to seek the same client base, or could they branch out and develop different types of business opportunities that would benefit the company in the long run?" Francis, a licensing agent, found a way to tackle the lack of compensation her assistant requested and deserved. She knew her assistant felt slighted when she couldn't get the raise approved, so she gave her an expense account with a spending limit that equaled the nonexistent bump in salary that management had blocked. As she said, "I wanted to reward a job well done, with the authority I had." Finding creative ways to mediate tough situations is the trademark of a good Queen.

• *Work toward making collaborative decisions that are more productive than just a mandate in a vacuum.* While you may need to mediate different points of view, you will have more to draw from, and people will feel they are being heard. Good Queens seek to involve others in the process, including peers, subordinates, and others who have a stake in the decision. Be mindful, though; you don't want too many cooks in the kitchen, and you don't want to give away your power. By delegating tasks and listening to others' opinions, you can earn respect and loyalty. "Anytime I involve employees in a decision or share my reasoning with them, they feel more involved, they understand why I'm doing what I'm doing, and they may even feel they have more of a share in the outcome," Tricia, a principal of a health product company, said.

• *Delegation can be a form of knighthood—you are bestowing a loyal supporter with a new responsibility and a way to serve the greater good.* Look at the tasks on your plate. Delegate the ones that are no longer honing your skills to see if those skills can be developed in someone else. Share the responsibility with an eager colleague, and they will become more experienced, appreciate the trust you have in them, and may even have a beneficial new perspective. "I had the greatest boss, she always gave me a shot with taking on clients I was passionate about," said Gwen, a talent agent. "If I showed enthusiasm, she would always take a minute to ask about my ideas, and very often passed on duties that she could have kept as her own but knew I might be interested in. Some of my colleagues experienced the opposite, and didn't have half the respect or loyalty for their management." Not only can you earn favors by delegating your tasks, but the more people who have a stake in your efforts, the better.

DISCIPLINE #2:
THE QUEEN IS PART POLITICIAN
AND PART ACTRESS

The Queen campaigns for her role as leader—she's a savvy politician. She knows she deserves the throne, but she also knows she needs to make her right to that exalted perch clear to everyone. There are many levels to a campaign—from the way you hold your head high during daily interactions, to actively canvassing for a promotion by increasing your platform and face time with "dignitaries." After you win your empire, as the Queen you've got to wear your crown well, and continue to cultivate an image as a royal who deserves to be respected.

NETWORK YOUR WAY TO THE CORNER OFFICE

Networking can raise your profile if done properly both inside and outside the office. It can open new doors for business development and potential new jobs, or forge important relationships. There is great truth in the cliché "It's not just what you know, but who you know." Schmoozing with people in power and networking through memberships in associations and organizations that are relevant to your industry are good ways to hold court outside the office. These campaigning activities will help you expand your reign—not just inside your company but outside as well.

A film/literary agent's assistant, Kim, decided to start sponsoring her own networking gatherings at a local restaurant with all the other assistants in the industry. "I wanted to get more contacts than my daily interactions were affording me." She went through her boss's Rolodex and invited all his colleagues' assistants, with his blessing. Socially, she had a great time, and quickly got to know them, and gained an immediate reputation as a leader and Queen with a lot of future players in her industry. She proved that holding court can be done regardless of position. There are so many websites these days that allow professionals to meet and connect. Check out websites like linkedin.com, friendster.com, myspace.com, ryze.com, gather.com, and meetup.com, or look for other websites that suit your field.

Be discreet. You don't want your political aspirations to be too obvious by trying too hard to gain exposure and connections. Surveyed executives made distinctions among doing a good job as a leader, searching for the spotlight, and finding a balance between the two. Regina Egea, currently vice president at AT&T in Bedminster, New Jersey, said, "There's a difference in my mind between seeking the limelight and their work shining through when you need certain contributions."[3]

While you want to get recognition, you don't want to be a credit hog. Otherwise, you might end up in the public eye for the wrong reasons or seem a little too desperate for stardom. How do you create balance as a good networking Queen? Create a personal elevator pitch that highlights your talents but isn't too hard a sell. I tell people to join Dale Carnegie or Toastmasters to develop their persona. Don't be shy—if you're a little scared of getting out there and strutting your stuff, there are plenty of resources (try fastcompany.com, careerjournal.com, and webgrrls.com) to help you enhance your "brand" as you make your way to the throne.

STEP ON THAT SOAPBOX!

Accept speaking engagements when you get the opportunity. As you address audiences more, the number of requests will grow, and so will your reputation if you truly have something to say. Elizabeth started her own leadership coaching business, and was giving seminars to groups of forty a year ago; now she speaks to groups of a thousand. As her lecture schedule increases so does her skill and her profile. "Every time I speak, I get a little better, even if it doesn't always go exactly like I want it to."

If you have a particular item on your agenda that you need to gain support for, jump on your soapbox and make yourself visible. Write opinion-based editorials, columns, or letters to the editor that pertain to your particular field. Just as the good politician makes her

3. Perri Capell, "Keep Your Career Moving by Raising Your Profile," *Career Journal*, May 26, 2004, http://www.careerjournal.com/myc/climbing/20040526-capell.html.

agenda known, doing this in a strategic way can build a platform for your campaign.

One smart, young PhD from NYU, named Chloe, said of writing and speaking, "I had been writing academically for most of my career, which is what most of my colleagues do, but recently, I began writing for commercial magazines and newspapers as well. It has broadened my appeal as a professor who can speak another language other than academia. It paid off; I just became the youngest tenure-track professor, and [the] only woman in my department. Now all the men look to me for direction."

THE QUEEN ACTIVATES GRASSROOTS SUPPORT

Tracy, vice president of an entertainment company, wanted to get to the next level. She knew the current president was poised to retire, and she wanted his job. She was already an expert networker and public speaker; that was what had gotten her this far. Essentially all she had to do was employ a winner-takes-all approach, and use the Queen to gain the support of her core constituents. This consists of some key steps:

- *Know your political base.* Learn about the departments in your company that you're not familiar with, and become actively involved with their constituents. "When the president of my company realized that I knew not only all of the heads of the departments in the company, but also the staff in the back warehouse who ran the production machines—he knew I was ready for an executive position," said Shane, a director at a printing company.

- *Everyone is a potential voter.* Until you get that position (or whatever goal you're shooting for), *don't offend anyone.* By ensuring that you have no enemies, only friends, you construct a track record that basically ensures your good standing as a Queen. If you want them to re-elect you, *show* them why they should and how you'll be when they do.

- *Get on the campaign trail.* Attend the meeting that's "optional," go to that after-work-drinks date, make sure you've got an invite for that special corporate event, and offer to be on the committee for industry functions. Join professional groups and online communities relevant to your field. Until you get where you want to go, don't stop politicking. The more public appearances and opportunities you have to present your agenda, the better.

- *Blog your heart out.* Provide commentary or news on your profession or industry, but don't become an exhibitionist—or escribitionist!

Tracy used these as the guiding principles of her campaign. She figured out that just by attending all of the monthly departmental meetings, she could expand her working knowledge, gain some face time, and get chummy with her political base. The employees in each division—from marketing to production and sales—saw her learning about the intricacies of each arm of the company and knew she wouldn't be just a figurehead Queen. When they pulled out the red carpet for a big client or a junket, she was there, shaking hands and taking names, and she handed out favors and promised loyalty to influential parties. Within six months, she was the favored candidate, and got the position when the current president stepped down.

THE GOOD QUEEN GOVERNS WITH VIGOR THROUGHOUT HER REIGN

Cultivating an image that revolves around goodwill can command loyalty, respect, and catch the attention of supervisors and subordinates. The good Queen gets what she wants without backstabbing or complaining; the bad Queen doesn't inspire allegiance, faith, or trust from her peers. We all know good Queens and bad Queens. Remember how you have felt about a bad Queen in your past. Do you want anyone to feel that way about you? I rest my case. Tap into the thespian within to keep up your political campaign, even after you've reached your goal—a Queen is always onstage.

There are high and low levels of acting and campaigning. As Queen, you want to be mindful of others' perception of your rule. Every interaction you have at work builds character; decisive actions and considerate gestures are important. People genuinely appreciate acts of kindness, however big or small. Your team might put a lot of effort into making things happen under deadline pressure, and when you show your gratitude, it reminds them that you value them.

"I always have my own employee appreciation day . . . my way of saying 'thanks for working so hard.' It's good for morale for them to know I think about them. We go to a nice dinner, and I report the big accomplishments for the company that year. I also try to give really good bonuses twice a year. Usually I try to do this in the summer, so it doesn't get confused with the holidays. I do something else for Christmas," says Jennifer, owner of an independent film company.

When a good Queen demonstrates her fair rule, she may be paid with undying loyalty—a valuable commodity for a successful business. And when she makes mistakes, she can admit them and move on rather than become defensive, angry, or blame it on those around her. She inspires the same sense of responsibility and candor in her colleagues. *The key to being a good Queen is always remembering that it is your ability, coupled with the ability of others, that allows you to achieve the success you desire.*

Interviews of successful leaders revealed that good leaders who earn respect from their employees make them feel safe from needless blame or dangers outside and inside the workplace.[4] As a good Queen, that should be your aim: to promote and protect your queendom. "I was so loyal to my boss—she always took the blame if our department made mistakes, and then she might have a private conversation with whoever was truly at fault," said an event coordinator. "We all appreciated it."

RULE #2:
IMAGE AND ATTITUDE AWARENESS ARE KEY

As a Queen you've got to be totally aware you're representing power, entitlement, and confidence. Know what you're projecting to the world. Consider the following image-building techniques to achieve your status as a Queen:

4. Martha Beck, "Good Boss, Bad Boss," *O, the Oprah Magazine* (January 2005): 5.

WEAR A CROWN. Check your posture. Is your head high, are your shoulders back, and is your chin up? Queens don't slump or use lazy body language or act distant and unapproachable. While you want to be a Queen of the people, walk like you've got a crown on your head. Just thinking to yourself *I need to be confident* doesn't cut it. Have conviction and express it nonverbally as well as verbally.

MAKE A ROYAL ENTRANCE. Do you command a room when you enter or do you morph into a wallflower? Notice whether or not you project confidence and a formidable presence when you need to command respect. Remember, the Queen is always in a royal state of mind. "Instead of grabbing a seat in the back of the room, I like to stride up to the front of a room or the head of the conference table for meetings or lectures," said Linda, a financial manager and Queen-in-training.

CONSTRUCT YOUR POLITICAL IMAGE. Don't be shy—be deliberate. Keep reminding yourself that you deserve that position and convey that with your energy and star quality. If you want to be a leader, you need to act like you already are one.

DRESS TO IMPRESS. A Queen doesn't wear jeans and flip-flips on casual Friday. She is prepared when the company president comes in on his day off or a special client drops by unannounced. The Queen always looks the part. "I always think to myself when I'm getting dressed in the morning; would I want to be seen by my top client or give a presentation in this outfit?" Mandy, an insurance vice president, said.

An article in the *Washington Post* noted that political Queen Condoleezza Rice's clothes were a combination of sex and power that was carefully considered. "Rice boldly eschewed the typical fare chosen by powerful American women on the world stage. She was not wearing a bland suit with a loose-fitting skirt and short boxy jacket with a pair of sensible pumps. She did not cloak her power in photogenic hues, a feminine brooch, and a nonthreatening aesthetic. Rice looked as though she was prepared to talk tough, knock heads, and do a freeze-frame *Matrix* jump kick if necessary."[5] You don't have to necessarily dress in ass-kicking sci-fi garb, but you need to cultivate your image. Rice is a pro at this.

STRUT YOUR STUFF WITH A SIGNATURE STYLE. A fashion statement can help a Queen build a unique persona—you can signal your distinctive style and colorful personality. Anna Wintour has her dark sunglasses and banged bob, Phillip Block is never seen without his Kangol cap, and Diane Keaton is known for her eccentric wardrobe. Drawing attention to something you're wearing can help you make your mark. You can spice up your look by making subtle or dramatic changes—anything from bright suits, distinctive haircut, funky glasses, or bold jewelry.

One talent agent, Betsy, who always has eye-catching (dyed) red, red, red hair said, "I'm a person who has tried every shade. I always wanted a lot of color in my hair because I wanted to stand out. I like to go for classic beauty mixed with over-the-top glamour. I'm so pale, red seems to work the best . . . women love it. They ask me about it all the time. I've come to find that my hair is the ultimate accessory."

5. Robin Givhan, "Condoleezza Rice's Commanding Clothes," *Washington Post*, 25 February 2005, C01.

Another Queen wore turtlenecks all year round, and still another favored men's pantsuits. Women who know how to use their flair to signal their power, are always remembered for that very thing. Just as Katie Couric is known for her fabulous shoes, some women always wear all black or favor silver over gold earrings.

- *Find your signature accessory.* This can be anything! It can be your sense of humor, your grandmother's broach, your baby-blue-colored contact lenses, your stilettos, your favorite colors, your hairstyle, or your belts. Don't hide your urge to put it out there and show it off.

DOMMERCISE:

Consider what traits your coworkers might mention if they were describing you. Are you happy with those hypothetical descriptions? Do you want to change that image you've consciously or unconsciously constructed? If so, modifications and enhancements are in order.

DISCIPLINE #3:
THE QUEEN IS AN EMPIRE BUILDER

The Queen has an eye on her legacy. Always searching for new territory to conquer, she considers her future, decides what she wants, and then makes it happen. In her search for ways to expand and grow her queendom or empire, she seeks to leave her mark on the world and gather a following.

YOUR CAREER COMPASS SHOULD BE FIXED ON YOUR LONG-TERM GOALS

In order to achieve your life's ambition, you must always keep in mind what it is you ultimately want. Are you in advertising but want to cross over to producing television shows? Do you work for a bank, but want to start a portfolio-management business? Is your current job a stepping-stone or a detour steering you away from the job of your dreams? I'm not talking about what you want your department to accomplish in six months, but rather your crowning achievement. When you retire, during the farewell wine-and-cheese party in the conference room, what will your peers say about your accomplishments? If you don't like where you're headed now, take the initiative to change course.

"When I really considered my career, I realized it wasn't in casting commercials, it was in creative development of films and commercials. I immediately began looking for a job writing and producing. I got one, worked hard, was promoted, and learned what it was all about. I then realized I was ready to move on to directing commercials. Now that I'm head art director, I enjoy what I do, and I couldn't have done it without those other experiences. But if I had just stayed in those jobs, and not explored other areas, I never would have gotten where I am today. Also, I couldn't have done it without carefully weighing my future goals, either." says Queen Lavinia. Always be aware of the next level and investigate ways of getting there.

Martha Stewart is a great example of a Queen who built an empire with ever-expanding long-term goals. She began as a caterer, and then expanded her brand to include books, television shows, magazines, merchandise—even home building is part of her queendom.

Susan Arnold, currently the highest-ranking executive in Procter & Gamble's one hundred and sixty-eight years, is the first female vice chairman. How did she achieve this position? Creative, innovative long-term thinking helped her make Procter a success in the beauty business after acquiring Clairol. She led her queendom to the cutting edge by learning how to identify with the largest P&G customer base—consumers on a limited income. She showed up other executives by leaving her comfort zone to find new territory. She had her staff live on a fixed income of sixty dollars a week for two weeks. A true Queen, she did not issue a decree that she herself would be excluded from. Following the rules herself, she did things like fill up her gas tank half full so she could afford shampoo and conditioner. It's this type of creative leadership that helped her push her way into the beauty business (a new direction for P&G), alongside other major players like Estée Lauder and Avon.[6]

6. Sarah Ellison, "The Top Women in Line to Lead," *The Wall Street Journal*, 1 November 2005.

Accurately reading the trends helped Susan figure out what could be improved upon in the lower, more economical beauty product market. Like her calculated push into new markets, you have to be creative, shake things up, and blaze a trail that hasn't been tried before. As a Queen, you must ask yourself: How can I expand my sphere of influence?

The Queen does not get caught up in the day-to-day minutiae and lose sight of the big picture. Her strength lies in remembering that her ultimate goal is to expand her reign and sovereignty. Each alliance, each step, and each day are building blocks that require vision and objectivity to accomplish what is truly best for the queendom. The Queen's advancement goals must always be at the forefront of her consciousness. Tapping into her ambitious nature and staying focused, she keeps her objectives in mind at all times and asks, "How will this action contribute to my long-term success?"

As Kira, a senior editor for a national magazine, said, "Even when I was an assistant, I tried not to let the daily workload sidetrack my goal of a promotion and greater responsibilities—in fact, that's how I got through some of the drudgery. It didn't seem as dull if I thought about it as a step toward something more." Everything you do is preparing you for something bigger and better.

Andrea, a newly appointed executive managing editor of a media company, said, "When my boss came to me and confided that he wanted to expand the company and start doing audio publishing, I was thrilled, since I listen to books on CD all the time at the gym. Though I had suspected it might happen, it caught me by surprise." The timing was right for her to tell him her ideas about reorganizing the company's book and magazine group to accommodate this new venture so she quickly put together a business plan.

"I went in the next day and told him that I thought I could make a major contribution to the new audio division, and suggested some ideas about consolidating the overlapping responsibilities between departments." Andrea gave him her outline, and the boss was very impressed with her moxie. Andrea was put on a team to launch the audio publishing program, which eventually led to a promotion and raise. If Andrea had hedged, or not had a vision of how the new division might fit into her future plans, she might have missed out. Instead, she's enjoying her new position.

RULE #3:
KEEP YOUR CARDS
CLOSE TO YOUR CHEST

Hopefully by now you're drawing up your blueprint for the new empire you will someday rule (or to an empire you're already ruling that you want to improve). What do you do with these oh-so-precious plans? Keep them to yourself.

Sometimes future prospects fall into the less-is-more category. You don't want the entire department to know you're eagerly awaiting the chance to be their boss. Have a few select confidants—but be very careful. If Andrea had blabbed her plans all over the company, they probably wouldn't have had the same impact. As

Andy Grove, senior advisor to executive management at Intel, once said, "Only the paranoid survive."

Miranda had a great idea for an op-ed piece in the local paper. She told an acquaintance in her writers group, and the next thing she knew, there was an editorial in the paper with a similar slant. "I felt so betrayed! Luckily for me, the person pulled it off the wrong way and didn't get much reader response mail."

When you are smart and clever, and you want to broadcast it to the world, watch out who you share your grand plan with. Everyone wants to get ahead; not just you. Good ideas aren't trademarked.

THE DARK SIDE OF THE QUEEN

Power tends to corrupt; absolute power corrupts absolutely.
—Lord Acton

Evil Queens are impatient, ruthless, and aggressive—they are drunk on their position power. Allison, a certified public accountant, told me, "My former boss berated me for siding with a client who was unhappy when gross errors were discovered on the tax return she prepared." Basically, Allison's boss saw her as disloyal and "borderline insubordinate," and put her on probation. The "off with their heads!" approach of a Gladiatrix does not go over well or encourage devotion.

I would advise women in Allison's position to be cautious when speaking truth to power, particularly with Queens like this, who blame others for their inadequacies. Allison found another job with a firm that knew about her former Queen's mixed reputation.

DOMMERCISE: Downtime

Strengthen your Queen by playing strategy games: Risk, chess, checkers, or backgammon. You'll learn planning, long- and short-term thinking, and patience. You will also bolster your competitive edge.

Now that you know how to wear that crown, I'll introduce you to the Governess, who's a whiz at making sure your queendom runs properly.

CHAPTER FIVE
ARCHETYPE THREE: THE GOVERNESS

WHAT'S YOUR SUPERVISORY MIND-SET?

Let's examine your abilities as a mentor and disciplinarian. Take a look at the statements below and rate yourself between 1 and 10. The higher you rate yourself for each statement below, the more accurate each statement describes you. You . . .

1. are passionate about coaching and enjoy learning. _____
2. understand the upside of praise and the downside of punishment. _____

3. are a stickler for time management. _____

4. enjoy problem solving and look for shortcuts without sacrificing quality. _____

5. inspire the personal best in others by doing the right thing. _____

If most of your answers are below 6, you need to brush up on your Governess skills. This chapter will show you how to get things neat and tidy. If you measure up, a refresher course can't hurt.

The Governess is a good mentor. She leads by example and stresses attention to detail and strong interpersonal skills. She doesn't cross the line; she draws the line. Like a good au pair or teacher, she lays down the law for the good of the whole team and keeps careful watch over form and function. She inspires appropriate behavior and provides a flawless example of organization in motion.

The Governess can also be a strict disciplinarian. Think of *Nanny 911*, except this Governess is the pedagogue of the office. She minds the rules and makes sure others abide by them too. She's a company gal—she doesn't challenge authority, and she sets up the systems that support management. Her knowledge of boundaries, manners, and protocol provides guidelines for good character and success. Sharing and expanding her knowledge is part of this officious role.

GET IN A GOVERNESS STATE OF MIND WITH EXPERT AND REWARD POWERS

In every job that must be done, there is an element of fun.
You find the fun and snap, the job's the game.
—Mary Poppins

The Governess is a well-worn, richly historical role that many domi-natrices embrace. Think of the most stern teacher you might have had saying, "Naughty, naughty!" As Mistress Lorelei says, "[The Governess's] success is not dependent on elaborate scripts, fine costumes, or other paraphernalia. To be a good Governess, you must supply chastisement. That's it."[7]

When someone has misbehaved or broken the rules, the Governess is there with a steely glare, upbraiding her charge. For the Corporate Dominatrix, the Governess is the ultimate headmistress. She keeps order, runs a tight ship, and provides intellectual stimulation and problem-solving support.

The Governess is also the keeper of expert and reward power: If you do your job well and meet deadlines, this sister might grant you something of material or personal value—a salary increase, promotion, extra vacation time, a bonus, or personal days. Expert power comes from experience, skill, and mastery. The Governess may be an expert in her field (or may work hard to become one) and designates herself as the person in charge of training coworkers and passing on her scholarship to others. In doing this she builds her company's knowledge and resource base.

---

7. Mistress Lorelei, *The Mistress Manual: The Good Girl's Guide to Female Dominance* (Oakland, CA: Greenery Press, 2000).

DISCIPLINE #1:
THE GOVERNESS IS A MULTITASK MISTRESS

The Governess knows how to make the trains run on time, as well as provide a smooth ride. She is motivated by a sense of duty, and possesses a keen awareness of human relations. She respects and creates organizational systems and makes sure they function. The Governess doesn't hesitate to provide constructive criticism *and* positive feedback. She rewards a job well done.

When Rachel, a librarian for an international architecture firm, started her job, the archives were in total disarray. The head architects or their assistants would go to the files, find what they needed for a presentation to a client, and shuffle through photos and slides without returning anything to where it belonged. For an influential firm, they were sorely lacking in functional systems. "I felt like I had walked into a major disaster!" she confided to me.

I told her to call in the Governess and take charge, rather than allowing herself to feel overwhelmed. She began by researching other architectural libraries to make sure she understood the best way to organize the material. Once she had a plan of action, she cataloged the assets by geographic location and made sure the labels had the name of the architect, date, and the name of the building. "Then I put together a manual that everyone in the company needed to follow when they wanted to use photos and slides. They had to sign each slide in and out, and put each one back where it belonged, according to its label." It worked like a charm.

In a managerial or administrative capacity, the Governess excels when creating structure and assigning tasks for herself and others. This can apply to everything from coworker coordination to late mail delivery. She doesn't ignore problems; she seeks solutions. To help her check off tasks, she always keeps a handy list. The Governess:

- works to set up training programs and improve skill levels of employees. She's always making sure that all her students are well educated.
- detects faulty systems and troubleshoots them. All the office functions get the white glove test; the broken ones do not gather dust.
- assigns tasks when there is a job to be done. Taking action instead of theorizing, she doesn't let her colleagues veer off track. As Ben Franklin said, "A little neglect may breed mischief." And the Governess will not stand for idle workers.
- keeps records and grids of deadlines, events, and procedures (diyplanner.com can come in handy). She knows her schedules and cut-off dates, and always maintains a paper and e-mail trail.
- updates her calendar regularly (micro to macro—personal and professional). The Governess doesn't forget lunches, meetings, conference calls, anniversaries, or birthdays.
- evaluates her progress and that of her peers in constructive, clear terms. Communication and accurate portrayal of expectations is the name of the game with this gal. If she doesn't think you're doing a good job, she'll let you know. If you deserve a pat on the back, you'll get one (maybe two).

The Governess has a to-do list of what, when, where, and how things are going to be taken care of—she might even use tadalist.com. She knows the rules, and sticks to them. If rules are unknown, she works on developing them to make them known in a fair and judicious fashion. We all have to be the Governess to get ourselves organized and focused on tasks.

Dixie, an executive director of a production company, lives by her schedules. She is a quintessential Governess. "Whenever I have multiple projects—a film, commercial, or TV show to work on— I'm in charge of the time line and when certain people are needed and when they are not. In the beginning, I tried to keep track of things on a simple calendar, but soon found that wasn't sufficient." After a struggle with trying to find the right system, she discovered the perfect computer program. Now she customizes grids for each production, with built in places for notes, so she can stay on top of details.

Not everyone will have the kinds of organizational demands that Dixie does, but it's good to note that sometimes you may need to do some research on different ways to manage your responsibilities, beyond just keeping a PDA. (Lifehacker.com is an excellent source of organizational information.) Each field is different, and each person has a particular system that works for them. As Joyce, an executive secretary, said, "Whenever I feel overwhelmed with the amount of tasks, I just write everything down and systematically check it off my list."

The Governess can help with making distinct administrative or task management adjustments. Sometimes you need to look at what is not working, and provide a new structure that will accommodate workflow. As one processing manager, Melinda, said, "customers didn't understand why, when they placed a work order, it always missed their estimated date of arrival. Everyone was scapegoating everyone else." After some investigation Melinda found out that the departments didn't know how long it took for work orders to be processed and how far in advance shipping orders needed to be placed. She held a company-wide meeting to institute a whole new set of procedures, then documented and distributed them. Accounts got their orders on time, and a real team spirit was activated.

Amanda, a nurse, was testing a vaccine for a pharmaceutical company and had to start the clinic for that research from scratch. She had to create a working system to keep track of the patients' files. "Until I devised a way to record the necessary information, it was chaotic. I had to organize how to input data, where we would store the results, and format the forms we would use to document any improvement." When asked the secret to her success, she said it's all about being consistent with her tracking system. "There's no other way I would be able to stay on top of it all." Establishing guidelines can save hours of stress, maddening paper searches, and your overall sanity. These systems are at the heart of the Governess's flair for organization.

ALWAYS ON THE LOOKOUT FOR THE NEW NEW THING

The Governess is naturally interested in strengthening her company's growth and productivity. "If my company is just selling to the same buyers, and producing the same products, I feel like we're not increasing our competitive edge. I enjoy researching fresh ideas and cutting-edge ways of doing things to see if there are opportunities our chief executive officer would be interested in," said Kirsten, a vice president of a health product company.

Launching new products or services, investigating new markets, and pulling all the initiatives together are tasks that the Governess knows how to tackle. She's the shining example to emulate when you're ready to gather intelligence and strike out in a new direction.

Rachael, a product developer for a toy company, wanted to add a new doll to her line, and the company president was open to her input. She prepared a proposal detailing all of the resources that would be required to produce the prototype—the costs and the potential marketing and distribution methods. "When I gather information about producing a new product, I try to explore every option, leaving no stone unturned—how much does it cost, and how much of a profit margin do we need to make it worth the effort. With the data that I collected for this particular product, I realized that we could outsource the design and production, and still make a profit."

The Governess has an affinity for research and development, because it straddles innovation and problem solving. R&D programs are the bread and butter of the future—a new market or product can make or break a corporation. Whether it's a new drug or new type of biofuel, giants like DuPont, BP, and Pfizer pour millions into research-and-development every year. It's essential for a business to survive when markets change and grow—this also makes the Governess an important player when evaluating where expansion will occur.

"I have to research first, before I implement any program that I do. That's the fun part, the learning part. The more information I collect, the better my decisions will be," one executive, Luna, said.

THE GOVERNESS IS A TROUBLESHOOTER

The Governess detangles situations that are complicated and fraught with subterfuge and finger wagging; she knows how to tell who is being naughty or nice. She takes it upon herself to separate the bad apples from the good. With her organizational tune-up, she'll get to the bottom of a situation, whereas her peers or higher-ups will seem to be chasing their tails.

Alice found herself in a tough situation when she took a newly created position as the director of customer relations. It was a small company, and most of the hiring had been done by the president of the company without well-documented job descriptions. The first thing she found was that people had fuzzy ideas about whose responsibilities belonged to whom—the director of shipping was pointing fingers at the production department, and the head of sales was giving unfair orders to the marketing department. Not only was it confusing, but the losing parties were the clients—their orders were being lost, and no one wanted to be responsible for the mistakes.

The Governess in Alice asked that everyone prepare job descriptions and evaluations for themselves and their colleagues, focusing on the question: How can we improve customer relations? After the appraisals were done, Alice recorded all of the feedback and gave a report to the president. "Everyone was forced to be very honest about what they felt customer relations entailed, and how good they were at it, and it revealed some management hiccups and a lot of interdepartmental overlap. They had to take a real look at what standards they had been creating for themselves and if those standards were effective or not."

The Governess's clarity, detail orientation, and follow-through can alleviate confusion. After reading Alice's final report, the president realized that departments needed to be reengineered. Hiring under vague job descriptions without the supervision of a Governess had bred a corporate culture where people didn't work and play well with each other. When one department doesn't know what the other is doing, it's a sign of what experts call the "silo," or "stovepipe," effect. As different parts of the company work in isolation or at cross-purposes, the business is compromised because of lack of cooperation, internal competition, communication breakdowns, and overall inefficiency. Alice was required to use the Governess role not only to make sure the right employees were servicing the right customers, but also to help them retain structure and accountability with deadlines, record keeping, and follow-up. Anytime you help establish or maintain corporate structure and create or follow standard procedures, you are using the power of the Governess.

This is an example of management issues the Governess can help with, but she can also be a saving grace with smaller stuff, such as day-to-day housekeeping. Assistants are often Governesses to a certain degree, making sure organization and support is there so their Queen or King can do her or his job. Rhonda, an executive secretary to a major chief executive officer, said, "I schedule his appointments for the dentist, doctor, accountant, and financial planner. Helping him manage his time better helps our department run smoother, because that's one less thing he has to think about."

RULE #1:
BECOME AN ORGANIZATIONAL WHIZ

Do you get buried under paperwork? Does your desk look like a tornado hit it? Take a moment to consider where the Governess's organizational skills may be used to your benefit. Think for a second: Who else makes your job possible? How would you function, for example, if your assistant's job was eliminated? How would you go about finding your files or keeping your calendar without him or her? Maybe a backup plan is in order. And if you are an assistant, who do you depend on—the mailroom, copy center, or the IT department?

Britney tried to move her Outlook contacts into her BlackBerry and did it incorrectly. The result: She lost everything—contacts, calendar, and notes. "It was terrible! I could have kicked myself." If she had foreseen the need for a backup system that was supporting her digital files, she'd have been a lot better off. Are you overly dependent on technology? If your computer crashes, have you backed up all your data? What can you do to strengthen your work efficiency?

One talent agent, Suzie, said of a job opportunity, "There was a terrific position up for grabs, and because it was so great, it went fast. I didn't have it together. I had to go home and revise my résumé and references, and when I finally found time to do that, they had already closed the position." Being ready for any opportunity in your career can turn out to be the difference between winning and losing.

Another way to keep yourself in check is to let the Governess visit your office every day. Set aside a few minutes in the morning or before you leave work to clean, file, organize, and follow up with loose ends. Returning phone messages, responding to e-mail, or making time to go through your in-box can clear your head and make sure nothing urgent gets lost in the shuffle.

One Governess, Ariana, said, "Whenever there are no more surfaces left to put files and folders on, I finally clean my desk and my office. I am forced to get organized, and when I'm finished, I feel much better." Try decluttering next time you feel like you don't know which way is up.

"I'm a control freak. I cannot tolerate a chaotic working atmosphere. An organized desk with a place for everything and everything in its place makes my work life more manageable; I know what I have to do for the day, I know where the materials are for me to accomplish those goals, and I'm always in the position to start new tasks on a fresh drawing board," Rochelle, a research specialist, told me. A messy desk makes for a messy mind, and an orderly desk makes for an orderly mind.

DISCIPLINE #2:
THE GOVERNESS IS A NATURAL MENTOR

All of us can look back and remember an influential, gifted instructor. Maybe it was a guidance counselor, a special teacher, a friend in school, or a generous, knowledgeable boss early in your career; they helped make us who we are. Advising a less-experienced colleague on how to get by successfully is an important discipline of the Corporate Dominatrix.

The obligation of instruction applies to all levels of an organization—whether you are a manager or a coordinator. An assistant can play the Governess with her supervisor to show her how to run a new computer program. The Governess is a useful role no matter what your position, since everyone has to mentor or teach someone at some point in their careers. Melissa, an architect, said, "I really appreciate it anytime my boss takes the time to walk me through something new, or even allows me to shadow her. She's a trusted advisor and it's seems crucial to have one to get to the next step in my career."

The Governess is particularly valuable in an environment of reorganization; restructuring; and what experts are calling "delayering," or taking the extraneous "layers" out of the corporate hierarchy. As a result, companies are asking managers to teach by example rather than carefully watching over every little move their employees make.[8] While this might be practical in some cases, mentoring is still essential for a well-trained, competent, loyal staff. Employees who get instruction, knowledge, and quality time with their bosses will be more in tune with what management needs, and they will make fewer missteps and not rely solely on trial and error.

Mentoring is more important than ever for women. Elizabeth Pagano, leadership coach and coauthor of *The Transparency Edge: How Credibility Can Make or Break You in Business*, said she finds that "mentoring is like good therapy as long as it's mentoring given by a dedicated leader. Their team will be more productive if they feel in touch, and trust that leader as a mentor."

8. Carol Hymowitz, "Today's Bosses Find Mentoring Isn't Worth the Time and Risks," *The Wall Street Journal*, 15 March 2006.

The Governess turns her workplace into a viable classroom, since it's important to the strength of her company; she's done her legwork and wants to pass on what she's learned. Studies reveal that having a mentor is a major key to a successful career. Shelia Wellington, the first woman to hold the position of secretary and vice president of Yale University, agreed. As more women advance beyond supporting roles into positions with more authority, the responsibility to mentor is greater. As women, we've got to be the ones to give other women at the bottom a boost through lending a helping hand. The Governess knows that we can't leave our own behind.

Mentoring is the Governess's strong suit; it is a core quality of the Governess that everyone should nurture. She does not dodge a colleague who needs a tutorial. She doesn't find excuses to avoid questions from people who need her support. Regardless of how many obligations she has in a day, she finds time to give professional advice, listen attentively, and keep confidences. By maintaining open lines of communication and seeking new sources of information, she encourages the growth of her peers.

One marketing director, Tammy, found that if she didn't invest time training her staff, she ended up spending hours putting out fires, and her department's work suffered. She realized that her job was easier when employees checked in on tough assignments rather than proceed when they were uncertain. "I feel more assured about what they are doing when they seek guidance. I would much rather interrupt what I'm doing and answer a question than stop what I'm doing and deal with a disaster." For Tammy, the Governess role gives her more confidence and she projects that to her direct reports.

THE GOVERNESS TRAINING CAMP

Taking time to be with colleagues one-on-one is great, but encouraging additional educational opportunities is also extremely worthwhile inside or outside your company.

One manager, Kim, an executive at an electronics firm, mentioned to me that she wanted to broaden the scope of her business. I suggested she do some research and encourage her employees to look at the competition and see where their services fell short. After the exercise, she came up with a novel idea. "I started a program in which we would pool resources with a company with a different product line on the West Coast (we're on the East Coast) so that we could benefit from their knowledge and they could benefit from ours. This company had mastered some of the customer relations strategies we were interested in, and we had an unusual business model they were curious about. We essentially traded information that benefited both companies." The result was a win-win for both sides, and Kim won praise for thinking outside the box.

RULE #2:
TAKE SOMEONE UNDER YOUR WING

In this fast-paced world of competitive business, we're all in a rush. It's still a good idea to take some time to show someone the ropes. This can be something as simple as taking time to explain how to use a new expense tracking system, or why one problem-solving approach might be more effective than another. Sharing your methods—from how you handle a tough situation with a client to how you put together a business plan or meeting agenda—can breed motivated employees. Consider the knowledge you have to pass on, and really try to employ the dexterity of a mentor when dispensing it to someone a little more green—the payoff could be big. Along with being a good teacher comes positive reinforcement and dedication.

One advertising director's assistant, Mary, said of her boss, "I would have never gotten my start if my boss hadn't taken a chance on me. I found a huge project, and he allowed me to represent it rather than taking primary ownership. It was a seven-figure deal, and it made my career." She now has undying loyalty to her boss and has been regularly contributing to his business. "He took the time to show me exactly how he would maneuver the deal, without being overbearing or condescending."

DISCIPLINE #3:
THE GOVERNESS BUILDS CHARACTER AND FOLLOWS CORPORATE ETIQUETTE

Like Emily Post, the Governess is always a lady using the proper etiquette. As Emily said, "Manners are a sensitive awareness of the feelings of others. If you have that awareness, you have good manners, no matter what fork you use." The Governess has that awareness *and* knows which fork to use. She understands that success takes more than just doing your job—you have to mind your manners, do what's expected of you, and then, take the time to show people how to do the right things the right way.

Building credibility and an honest reputation can take you places that expertise alone can't. Cultivating relationships and networking not only build character but can solidify connections with people who will appreciate your genuine effort, and may end up helping you down the road. These traits are "soft skills," like celebrating a birthday, as opposed to "hard skills," like budgeting or negotiating contracts. The Governess is necessary in grooming soft and hard skills. Being considerate can smooth the rough edges in employee-client relations; social graces reflect good form, which, in the long run, will set you apart from the rest. Some suggestions:

MIND YOUR MANNERS. Just as a Governess chides boys and girls to say ma'am and sir or please and thank you to get what they want, this discipline of the Corporate Dominatrix reminds you to make the extra effort with business contacts, colleagues, and clients. That means not just finishing a report or presentation and moving on to bigger and better things, but acknowledging coworkers who made a contribution, whether large or small. You want the people you deal with to have a good impression of you long after the deed is done.

"I always write a note, whenever I want to say 'thank you,' or remind someone it was terrific to meet them or do business with them. E-mail just seems too impersonal." Catherine, a life coach, makes sure that her clients or associates know she took a moment out of her day especially to correspond with them directly.

Gail, a wedding planner, used the Governess to help build her reputation with clients and found it really paid off. "I send handwritten notes with little gifts after every wedding to the parents and the bride and groom to say 'thank you for hiring me.' When selecting these tokens of appreciation, I keep my clients' personal interests and preferences in mind." By saying thank you, she also reminded her clients that she helped them make a magical day happen.

ARRIVE PREPARED AND ON TIME. This may seem like a very simple rule, but think about whether or not you are actually doing it. That habit of arriving ten or fifteen minutes late not only stresses you out, but it throws you off your game. Even though being fashionably late is accepted, your action is disrespectful to the party you're meeting. Try to be on time, and actually get there a few minutes early to gain an upper hand. You'll notice it will keep you calm, cool, and collected, and people will notice it. "I always get everywhere early, and now it's as much a habit as being late was. Now that I'm always on time, I get so irritated when others aren't. I just feel like they're being rude!" says Sally, a public relations director.

Besides just being on time, make sure you're prepared. Did you look at the material you're discussing and bring along appropriate show-and-tell items? Clear your mind and focus on the person and topic; giving your undivided attention shows respect and wins points.

TREAT EVERYONE EQUALLY. Don't ignore an assistant or a secretary when making a beeline to the bigwig in the corner office. Lucy, a practiced Governess, said, "I am always just as nice to the assistants as I am to their bosses when I call potential clients. Not only do the assistants move up the ladder and are potential clients of mine, but sometimes they have their boss's ear, too. When I call a client, I learn their assistant's name and establish a pleasant rapport with them. I've found they'll give me the inside scoop on the client's mood (is this a good day or a bad day?) and squeeze me in as a favor when I really need one." Practicing equality with people at all levels within a company will polish your reputation.

THE GOVERNESS DEMONSTRATES INTEGRITY THROUGH THOUGHTFULNESS

Alyson, a pharmaceutical rep, learned that being attentive went a long way. With dozens of reps dropping by her doctors' medical office all day, she had to make her mark through something besides simply schmoozing. "One physician really liked sushi, so I would arrive with a platter of exotic delicacies when we worked through lunch together. I always remember to ask about their spouses and children, by name. I actually sell more products and get more referrals than when I had not made that effort. A connection beyond business is created between us and it makes a difference."

All good salespeople know the power of persuasion. Every element of an interaction counts; it comes down to how far you are willing to go to extend yourself. Genuine actions go far with colleagues, customers, and clients. That's where the Governess plays an important role, she does what is required, no matter how tired, irritated, or overworked she might be. Even if you have the right product or a perfect presentation, you still need that personal touch to make an impression. The Governess builds solid relationships through:

- remembering faces and names, or the names of family members and favorite pets;
- keeping in mind if a client has a particular hobby and asking about it; and
- sending a card if you hear through the grapevine that someone experienced misfortune, isn't feeling well, or got a promotion.

Taking note of people's interests doesn't take a lot of time, just more attention. Part of your protocol as a Governess is to remember simple things about people that make a big impact. Doing a little research to find a client's favorite type of wine for a celebratory gift goes a long way, especially when the competitor just sends an e-mail to say congrats.

CAN YOU HEAR ME NOW?

In our increasingly global economy, familiarizing yourself with the mores of a different culture can help your business meetings and your presentations. For example, videoconferencing has grown in popularity in the past few years, thanks to less-expensive equipment. Many companies do videoconferences with foreign clients with very different backgrounds, so understanding and appreciating those differences is key. Thomas Zweifel, chief executive officer of Swiss Consulting Group and author or *Culture Clash: Managing the Global High-Performance Team*, gives the following "Dos and Taboos" of global citizenship[9]:

9. Thomas Zweifel, *Culture Clash: Managing the Global High-Performance Team*, Global Leader Series (New York: Select Books, July 2003), 40.

- Watch your hosts and do what they do.
- Never take English for granted. Remember that if English is not their first language, they make it work for you with every English sentence they speak or hear.
- Respect people, their ideas, and their cultures. Be polite, on your best behavior, not loud.
- Interact with people as individuals, not as culture. Resist the urge to generalize.
- Listen when people tell you all their issues. Listening is a vastly underrated skill. Resist the urge to immediately resolve the issues—hearing them is often enough to dissolve them.
- Be open to input and to learning. You can learn enormously from other cultures (both about [them] and yourself).
- Remember that understanding even one country or culture can be a quest of a lifetime. It is not something you can check off and be done with.
- Say so if you don't know. Don't wing it.
- Find the gate to the village if it is fenced in. Do *not* take the village by storm.
- Talk to someone who is clear whenever you are not clear. Keep a shared understanding with your partners on your mission.
- Remember that your advice is noise in their ears unless they want it.

Being aware of other people's dissimilarity will help you when you're in a professional situation with someone not just of a different culture but of a different generation. Older colleagues may not react the same as colleagues your own age. They may not appreciate getting an e-mailed contract back with tracked changes (a Microsoft Word feature that allows you to edit electronically instead of manually), and might prefer a hard copy with a letter instead. Keep in mind the comfort level of older, as well as younger, generations when the question of corporate etiquette comes up. "I had a boss who really felt like every client deserved personal correspondence in hard copies, updating them about their account, rather than e-mails with digital files or PDFs attached. That was his form of good corporate manners," one office manager, Tracy, said.

Weaving attention to detail into your daily routine will take you a lot farther than simply doing your bottom-line duties. The Governess can help you monitor your own behavior and keep you in line when you forget that every little gesture or appropriate action bolsters your professional standing.

RULE #3:
REACH OUT AND TOUCH SOMEONE

When you feel like dodging someone, or responding in a perfunctory way, think of the Governess shaking her head and chiding you: Is that good form? Here are some easy ways to display proper behavior in your day-to-day work life.

DON'T BE A STRANGER. Taking the time to connect in a fast-paced world means more than it ever did. Keep track of people who move up the corporate ladder in your industry, and stay in touch with them. While it might pay off, it also feels good to let someone know you're thinking about them. When you correspond regularly, people remember you. They appreciate the time you take to extend yourself.

DIRECT RESPONSIVENESS. "Blowing someone off" is not in the Governess's vocabulary. It's a good practice to respond to any type of overture. Never mind the awkward feeling when you see people and remember *you didn't* return their calls or e-mails. Getting back to people in a timely fashion is just good form. This is true, even if you inwardly groan when you get the message. One art director, Marsha, said of an executive, "I didn't return a call right away because I hadn't heard from this woman in a while, and the last time I talked with her she was looking for a job. I thought she might be calling me to pick my brain about opportunities. When I finally called her back a week later, I found out that she had landed a senior director position and was looking to hire a right-hand woman— me!" You never know who might be instrumental in your next career move, so treat everyone the way you'd like to be treated. Even if someone doesn't seem like a mover and shaker now, they may be one in the future.

THE DARK SIDE OF THE GOVERNESS

Tormenting (or tormentoring) instead of mentoring is a danger for a Governess. One publicist, Mandy, said of her hypervigilent and obsessive boss, "Every time the phone would ring I would jump because I knew it might be my account manager, calling me into her office to nit-pick about something I had done or not done. Essentially her message was 'You don't measure up and you're not smart enough.' Everyone in our department was treated this way. I never felt secure enough to make good decisions." Now Mandy has a job at a competing company, and was quickly promoted to publicity manager. Her confidence returned as did her ability to do excellent work. Unfortunately her old boss weakened the department's effectiveness by too much absolutism.

Any department, company, or individual is more efficient when there is a continuous process of training and development. You will be contributing to your future and the future of others when you share and exchange knowledge and experience with colleagues and customers alike.

DOMMERCISE: Practice Makes Perfect

Consider babysitting or become a Big Sister to a needy child. Minding and mentoring children will put you in the position of the natural Governess.

Now that you've learned how to master the functions that keep a company running, let's move on to the warrior woman, the Amazon.

CHAPTER SIX
ARCHETYPE FOUR: THE AMAZON

WHAT'S YOUR MERCENARY MIND-SET?

Let's see if you have what it takes to be a soldier of fortune. Take a look at the statements below, and rate yourself between 1 and 10. The higher you rate yourself for each statement below, the more accurate each statement describes you. You . . .

1. believe the best offense is a good defense. _____
2. are comfortable debating the issues and understand that conflict goes along with change. _____
3. learn from your miscalculations and mistakes. _____
4. buck bureaucracy when necessary. _____

5. regard a bit of paranoia as necessary; victory is temporary; and you must always be on your guard. _____

If most of your answers are below 6, you need to learn the military methods of the Amazon. This chapter will show you the ropes. If you think you're a natural warrior, you may still need a battle plan!

We've all heard of the legendary Amazon women. Consider the bold attitudes of Ann Coulter, Camille Paglia, or Arianna Huffington to get the flavor of this sassy, determined sister. She speaks her mind and utilizes courage to get her way. From Joan of Arc to Xena, Warrior Princess, these strong-willed women don't back down from a fight, as long as it's worth the show of force. The Amazon defends what she believes in, providing she's in the right.

A mistress of game planning and combat maneuvers, she's a formidable lady and generally a force to be reckoned with. Independent, heroic, and fearless, she leads her comrades into battle with bravery and resolve. Facing down any dissenters with conviction, she stands firm and resolute when confronted with anything that won't lead to victory.

GET IN AN AMAZON STATE OF MIND WITH COERCIVE POWER

Don't confuse defending yourself with using a weapon. When you pull your sword, you have to be ready to kill.
—Xena in "Dreamworker," from *Xena: Warrior Princess*

The Amazon embodies many of the characteristics of a military strategist. She understands the subtle forms of coercive power that employ manipulation and display intent through verbal facility, body language, and readiness to do what she has to do.

Coercive power is not to be used just because you feel angry, hurt, slighted, or maligned; it is to be used *only* when all other approaches, including diplomacy, fail. It is a last resort to settle a situation that is not working or is unjust. This type of power involves "forcing" (and I use that term delicately!) someone to go along with your program, providing it makes good business sense. The operative principle of the Amazon is to *use might, but only when you're in the right*. Coercive power is not only used to declare war, it's also used to keep the peace. In the case of the Corporate Dominatrix, keeping the productivity *and* the profits going is paramount.

The Amazon knows that if she can get others to do her bidding or acknowledge her strength, she will very often gain control. As a boss, this can take the form of fighting for more staff and internal resources or bigger budgets. As a subordinate, taking on the Amazon role when interacting with a supervisor is a delicate issue—it involves standing up for your rights and understanding what the repercussions of that act might be.

The Amazon fantasy is about conquest: back straight, chin up, with an assertive, commanding presence. She is what one popular S&M fantasy denotes as a "leatherwoman," clad in skins from head to toe. Like the costumes she wears, she's tough, menacing, and poses a threat to anyone who doesn't obey; her armor is heavy and withstands assault. The Amazon isn't going to get her feelings hurt or accept setbacks easily. Modern Amazon warriors can be seen in the formidable female characters in movies such as *Charlie's Angels* and *Kill Bill*—hard-nosed women who fight for what they want and hold nothing back.

In relation to the Corporate Dominatrix, the Amazon wields her power forcefully and bravely, embodying many of the same characteristics as the Amazon role-played by mistresses. She conquers, kicks ass, and takes names (in a very figurative sense) whether she's championing an idea, standing her ground, or challenging authority. When a battle needs to be fought, she leads from a defensive or an offensive position, and is the first one on the battlefield. Her convictions are the knowledge she's in the right, the intent that the war is worth the potential casualties, and the understanding that the repercussion of her actions are not known for sure. Rather than tackling the opposition head-on like a bull in a china shop, she can attain her objective through artful, sometimes manipulative, gallant strategies.

DISCIPLINE #1:
THE AMAZON IS NOT DETERRED BY DEFEAT

Let's say you're struck with a brilliant way to develop a new business. You've thought things through, and your ideas are worth the commitment, time, resources, and energy. However, you're met with resistance or reluctance from management. You need a yes-man, and you've got a room full of naysayers. You know if they would just give you the green light, you could make magic happen. As the Amazon warrior, you may just succeed at what might seem like a mission impossible. This sister is not deterred by obstacles— she doesn't take no for an answer easily, and she will go back into the ring for what she believes in.

Barbara, a graphic designer, said, "I'm a very agreeable employee, but when I found that a better health plan was not one of my supervisors' priorities, I decided that something had to be done. I brought it up at a company meeting and got shut down immediately."

I told Barbara that it would be counterproductive to go in to oppose management in a blatantly confrontational way. She would need to build up internal support with employees, and make her case. The Amazon is a strategist, after all. She needed to maintain a positive attitude, even after a comeuppance. After talking to a group of her peers, Barbara persuaded them to submit the same requests for better healthcare to not only their supervisor but also their supervisor's supervisor. Coordinating her resources, she chipped away to make her objective a reality. After submitting multiple requests and vigorously following up, Barbara's supervisor got a reality check after six months—the demands for better healthcare weren't going to go away, so the boss asked the human resources director to analyze better healthcare programs.

The Amazon is a *V*-is-for-"victory" kind of gal—defeat is a temporary state. When she is beaten, the Amazon resorts to her resilience and tact to carry her past the disappointment. She uses her knowledge from her past experience to help her better plan for her next crusade.

A software developer, Anna, figured out a new menu of services she wanted to offer customers. After getting a little brush-off about it from her boss, she decided to see what other departments thought about it. She met individually with allies in publicity, marketing, and sales, and returned to her boss with everyone's positive feedback on the impact on their business. "I showed him how everyone else would support it and the potential revenue they had projected. He was impressed and gave me the go-ahead."

The Amazon finds other ways to make things work to her advantage if the first path is blocked. Mary, an event planner for a New York real estate development company, was in charge of running an outing in a new Southern territory—Nashville, Tennessee. After Mary and her staff for months planned an elegant outdoor garden party, disaster struck less than a week before the event. She called me in a frenzy because the weather forecast was calling for thunderstorms, and the jazz band was sick and couldn't make it. I told her she had a choice: She could allow herself to be defeated and cancel the event *or* she could slip into the Amazon role and find some alternative ways to make it work.

Mary needed to adapt to the changing conditions. After tons of calls, she found out that one of the agents in the company was in a bluegrass band—and they were available to play. Since the shindig would now be indoors, the renovated barn on the original property would work with the change in music. Mary didn't pitch the employee's band as simply a backup, but rather a good public relations ploy. She convinced her boss to move forward, and he rather reluctantly agreed. "Suddenly I pictured a whole different event— I went and bought gingham cloth, asked the florist to use sunflowers instead of lilies, and decided to serve BBQ instead of escargot and lobster. Within a few hours I had a hometown, country dinner planned—perfect for Nashville. It came off beautifully, and everyone had a great time."

The chain of events actually helped Mary plug into a whole new image for the company, opening the door for new clients. Her boss was glowing the next day, and reported that they had figured out how to stand out from the other competitors.

When the Amazon hits a landmine, she finds another unblocked road. When her basic strategy doesn't work, she searches for something else that does.

THE AMAZON IS THE ANTI-PUSHOVER

This lady doesn't take things lying down. Rather than just falling into line when something is unjust or when she's not getting the credit and respect she wants and deserves, she draws on her ballsy gumption to get what she needs.

One of my clients had to become an Amazon to make sure her job was secure. Christie, a magazine editor, told me, "My publisher has no children. I knew that she looked unfavorably at women who unplugged from the office when out on maternity leave. When I had my first child, I was not going to lose everything I'd worked for—I wanted to return to my job and my career."

Christie and I talked about what to do when she began noticing she had been left out of department e-mails that concerned her section of the magazine. Rather than consulting with her, the publisher was making decisions about her articles and handing off her duties to others. I told her to not accept defeat and to use the gutsy power of the Amazon in a direct, clear way. Her friends at the office were throwing her a baby shower, and I suggested she go to battle before the event to allow her work-oriented Amazon persona to over-shadow the maternal, personal role she'd be playing at the shower.

"The week before the shower, I called a meeting with all of the heads of departments, and invited the publisher too. I then told them that although I would be taking eight weeks of maternity leave, and I would be working from home part-time until I returned to the office officially. I expressed my intentions clearly, concisely, and made my point with everyone—I wanted them to know how much I cared for my job, and intended to be actively involved." She also presented a comprehensive plan for the content of the magazine each week she was away and blocked any attempt at a coup. "My publisher actually respected the point I made—and it worked. I'm the only person so far who has had a good, working relationship with the publisher after my baby was born!"

Katie had been working very closely with the chief executive officer of her company for seven years when, during his divorce, he made some inappropriate comments to her. "I was so mad; I had trusted him and now he was crossing boundaries! I didn't want to work with him anymore, and I was ready to strike out on my own." We put together an Amazonian game plan, and I told her to try to get compensation that would help cushion her new venture. She confronted him and said, "You and I both know how difficult it is to work under these circumstances, and I'd like to use this opportunity to invite you to make your company my first client." He agreed to six months' severance pay, and she left his company to start her own. He also agreed to act more professionally and see a therapist.

The Amazon puts the kabosh on being pushed around. When someone tries to rattle your cage, remember you don't reside in one. In some situations, you've got to demand respect and stand your ground. As one Amazon, Sandy, told me, "After years of hard work, I had finally reached senior editor at a major publishing house. This meant that I could hire my own assistant, and I began receiving résumés from the Human Resources department, to set up interviews. Word came down to me that someone in a very high position wanted me to hire a celebrity's kid for the job. I interviewed her, and she came across as [being] smug." This candidate also told Sandy she didn't have an interest in reading submissions or doing the typical job of an assistant. Whether someone had already promised her the job or not, this young lady had a strong sense of entitlement.

I told Sandy she couldn't roll over and hire this woman because of nepotism. She would be in for a lackluster assistant, and would always harbor bad feelings toward her boss. As Sandy told me, "The supervisor didn't want to hear my reasoning about not hiring her.

She finally stopped trying to be nice and looked me straight in the eye. 'Hire her,' she commanded. . . . I got real, real mad."

The Amazon was not going to stand for that! After she shook off her anger, Sandy approached the publisher near his office on a not so "chance" encounter. He asked her what was new, and she told him all about the unsuitable rich kid that she'd interviewed the day before. As Sandy said, "He knew exactly what I was up to, and my coincidental meeting didn't fool him one bit. I stood my ground and didn't budge. Finally he said, 'I understand.' And that was that—I hired someone else. My supervisor never mentioned it again."

Sandy prevailed. She checked in with the Amazon, rallied her courage, and proved that she had a spine.

THE AMAZON HAS STEEL COJONES

The Amazon is not only useful in the face of adversity; she also comes in handy when you need a little confidence and courage in day-to-day situations. When you're in a brainstorming meeting and you bring up a terrible idea (let's face it, we all have terrible ideas every once in a while), you may be hesitant to bring up another one. The Amazon doesn't bruise easily; she doesn't allow her confidence to be battered after just one misstep. She looks forward, not backward.

Melinda, a designer, wanted to bring a new line of accessories to market, but her director poked holes in her proposal. Rather than backing down, she decided to take the concept to a pitch meeting anyway. This was especially challenging because all the other attendants were her superiors and her boss might resent her chutzpah. Taking a deep breath, she made her case. "I just thought, to hell with it! If it flies, I just know this line of products will create a younger customer base."

The room listened intently, and afterward, her director predictably spoke up and sited several problems with Melinda's plan. Undeterred, Melinda proposed a few alternative solutions to overcome those weaknesses. The chief executive officer carefully mulled over the feedback, and then asked Melinda to submit the revised proposal directly to him, stating, "It has some merit; I'd like to think more about it." The Amazon had put her on the chief executive officer's radar, and on the road to her new line of accessories.

As Melinda discovered, the conviction an Amazon brings to a situation can breathe new life into a project or interpersonal exchange. People will perceive that you are not easily brushed aside, and they will respect your ideas even more than they might otherwise. When you meet opposition, carefully consider if you are passionate about what you want to accomplish, and go for it. The Amazon will see you through.

RULE #1:
PRACTICE HEALTHY FEARLESSNESS

The Amazon keeps her fears under control. Do you tie yourself up in knots over office politics, performance reviews, workplace pressures, increased responsibilities, and looming deadlines? Look within yourself to see if you operate in a cage of self-sabotage or inertia. Did someone tell you not to make waves? Attitudes like "men don't like women who are too successful" imprison us and inflict self-imposed limitations. As Karen LaPuma notes in her book *Awakening Female Power: The Way of the Goddess Warrior*, "Where we put our attention determines the nature of the experiences we draw to us. The amount of attention we give something is equal to the amount of feeling behind it. If there is fear present, it becomes an especially powerful web that ensnares us in survival, avoidance, and struggle. Our freedom comes by penetrating beliefs. Describe a belief and clear any strong emotions concerning it, and it loses its power."[10]

In speaking to working women at every level of management in companies large and small, I realized that women fall into three distinct varieties of boldness: functionally fearful, dysfunctionally fearless, and healthily fearless. Nancy, for example, is a stockbroker who was always worried that her job was on the line. Though her clients adored her, she always had the feeling the other shoe was about to drop. She was kind of like the kid who always thought she would fail, and then got an A. No matter how many A's Nancy received, she still fretted that a C was in her future. Nancy was functionally fearful, though she kept her anxiety from public view. She had found a way to accommodate her unease while still being productive.

One day I asked Nancy what would happen if she actually did lose a client, or worse, her job. Would she survive? Doing a worse-case scenario exercise was helpful. Once Nancy was able to let go

10. Karen LaPuma, *Awakening Female Power: The Way of the Goddess Warrior* (Fairfax, CA: SoulSource Publishing, 1991), 22.

of trying to control future events, she could relax and enjoy her successes without anticipating failures.

On the other hand, Lana, an entertainment lawyer, projected boundless self-assurance and energy. In fact, some people thought she was a bit full of herself. Though she is incredibly smart and accomplished, she would sometimes shoot from the hip, and didn't sweat the small stuff, which could be problematic in her profession. Oftentimes the devil is in those small details, and Lana had been caught missing some sticking points in important contracts. Lana was dysfunctionally fearless; she was flying by the seat of her Armani pants. It *is* possible to cut corners, but not in a reckless way that can bite you on the butt down the line. Lana needed to adjust her over-confidence and focus less on herself and more on her work. When she realized the dangerous game she was playing with her career, she modified her behavior and won over colleagues and clients alike.

Healthy fearlessness is leaving your comfort zone under opti-mal circumstances and trying something new—whether it is a job, a hobby, or a project. Janice, an engineer, went on an Outward Bound retreat with her company. Not terribly athletic or in shape, she really needed to push herself to participate in the exercises, including rock climbing and hiking. "It was difficult to see the benefits at the time, but I broke down boundaries and felt great," she said. Her colleagues were as surprised as she was at her ability to keep up.

I've found that women tend to want to be rewarded for a job well done but don't necessarily think they should ask for the reward or tell anyone what they think the reward should be. One leadership coach, Barbara Pagano, of Executive Pathways, told me, "I see women all the time who are fearless in their career and really ballsy when they need to be to achieve success in daily work, but they are not fearless when it's time to ask for a raise." It's a fact: Many women have a tough time asking for what they're worth. Because they work hard, they feel their performance speaks volumes. Deep down, some women even go so far as to think that asking for their reward is somehow rude or that you should graciously accept what you get without complaint.

We can all take a lesson from my mom. She always told me, "If you don't ask, you don't get." The worst that can happen is they say no. To ask, though, takes healthy fearlessness.

Another high-level achiever, Abbey, a senior executive at a financial firm, found out that a vice presidency she had long been promised was given to her two male colleagues instead. Incensed, she finally drew the line and had to shift into Amazon mode—she went home and told her boss she wouldn't come back to work until she got a title change. "It was hilarious, looking back, because he called me and said, 'Are you serious?' and I said yes! I was so pissed off!" Ultimately her boss impressed upon upper management to make good on their word after she completed work on a major project.

It's time to evaluate whether or not you're fearless in a healthy way. Are you a leader or a lemming when it comes to putting a price on your self-worth? Is there something you've been afraid to ask for? Want a bigger budget, a certain perk, or to move into that empty office with a window? Has your boss reneged on compensation promises? Become a black belt in corporate self-defense.

DISCIPLINE #2:
THE AMAZON IS BATTLE READY

While the Amazon is undeterred by setbacks, she does not run blindly into battle. This means that she is careful to prepare, to rally the troops, and to make sure her cause is just. The Amazon should always know what the repercussions of her quest will be—is she risking her job? Is she going to offend a valued boss or peer? Do the positive outcomes outweigh the negative? She picks her fights carefully and is fierce but not foolhardy.

Just because you're the Amazon doesn't mean you can act like a Gladiatrix. A Corporate Gladiatrix goes overboard by provoking management too much, overusing her attack mode, and picking her feuds unwisely.

THE AMAZON HAS AN EXIT STRATEGY

This warrior woman can find herself in pretty uncharted territory, and she always travels with a mental map, an internal compass, and a way out. The Amazon knows when to advance, but she also knows when to retreat.

"When I get outraged about something at work, I take a step back, and give myself a day to cool down before I rush headlong into something," one mergers and acquisitions consultant, Rebecca, said. "My job is to consult with people who are taking over companies, and there is a lot of room for blow-ups, even though many times success dictates that you remain aggressive. I always try to understand all the different ways things can fall apart. . . . It makes us all more prepared to deal with mishaps when we want to take over a company. If we need to pull out quick, I like to know what my options are."

Larissa was a manager in a branding company and had used her skills to develop an impressive roster of clients and projects. She had brought in hundreds of thousands of dollars for the firm, though she wasn't adequately compensated for her dedication to her job. She wasn't getting the bonuses she wanted, and a colleague, not half as accomplished, got a plumb promotion she felt she deserved. She needed to lay down the law with the owner of the agency and get her due, or come up with a Plan B.

I told her she could leave and begin her own agency, and probably make as much as she was making with this company, if not more. If she had already tried asking for a better compensation package and got sidelined, the only way she might be able to get what she deserved was to force a power play in a healthfully fearless way. Bottom line: She could either get her due or leave the company—with the profitable clients in tow. The first order of business before the showdown was to develop her departure strategy: Where would she establish her office and had she secured enough clients to take with her? She had secret talks with a few of her clients, and the big ones agreed to move with her. When she felt like she had her ducks in a row, she went in to give the ultimatum to her boss. She ended up feeling so good about her exit strategy that she decided to act on it, even though her boss was in favor of a raise. Staying at the company was no longer enough for her, and now she runs her own successful agency.

As a battle-ready Amazon, you need more than just gumption and blind bravery; you have to analyze the details of your mission and show evidence that supports your point of view or objective.

"After owning five small businesses, I don't charge into something and invest everything I have unless I've asked all the right questions, and know there is a very good chance of success. When I decide to start a new business, I want to know more about that venture than anyone else—what are the risks, what are the real margins of profit, and who are my competitors? I'm basically going to crush my adversaries; I have to have a different strategy than they do," said one expert warrior, Tricia, entrepreneur and owner of several restaurants.

As Sun Tzu says in *The Art of War*, "Warfare is the greatest affair of state, the basis of life and death, the Tao to survival or extinction. It must be thoroughly pondered and analyzed." Deliberation and strategy are essential to victory. No matter how courageous you may be, you must be smart about your attack, and analyze the possible outcomes.

War doesn't have to be about a major deal or department takeover; it can be just a simple conquest, or a tough discussion or confrontation. But in order to win, you must have logic behind the conquest. When the Corporate Dominatrix goes into high gear as an Amazon, she does her homework, she knows who her allies are, and she executes her battle plan in a smart, assertive, and savvy way.

Bethany, executive director of sales, was the head of a satellite office that handled new business for an electronics company. "I found out I would have to let two of my sales reps go because they recently lost a big client. As it was, my staff was stressed and overworked, but still generated revenue that exceeded expectations."

She worked on a presentation to her direct supervisor as a final plea to keep her staff. In order to prepare, she first compiled sales records from the past five years, and found that her team had actually helped the company grow overall by 15 percent. Second, she realized that if there were department cutbacks, there would be fewer employees to handle the accounts and they would do less soliciting for new business. Third, her plans to expand sales operations to the West Coast would be more difficult to implement if they were understaffed.

She went to headquarters to make the pitch in person and made sure that she looked the part by wearing a power suit. She carried herself in a self-assured way—she owned that room for the duration of her presentation. In her mind, she visualized having already conquered. The outcome: Her supervisor was so impressed by her gumption and documentation, he agreed to keep the employees on for one year as a trial.

With authority and skill, this Amazon left no stone unturned before a clash with the opposition.

RISK TOLERANCE

When you fight for something at work, you need to understand your own risk tolerance. Don't forget what's at stake. You need to assess before you charge headlong into the fray what's at risk if you do fail. If you're going up against management for a raise and putting everything on the line, do you have savings or a backup job in case they take a hard line? If you're investing everything you have on one venture, what resources do you have if it fails? In Bethany's case, the worst her supervisor could say was no, and she'd just have to let the reps go. She knew what her risk tolerance was for that situation. Before you begin a discussion, ask yourself if you can handle losing.

RULE #2:
MAKE SKILL AND PREPARATION YOUR WEAPONS OF CHOICE

Many military strategists have attempted to encapsulate a successful campaign into a set of principles. These rules of the road can help equip your Amazon for anything that comes your way:

- *Select decisive objectives.* Don't waffle about what you want; be clear about your goals whether that means beating out a competitor, getting a raise or promotion, or making a specific industry change.
- *Keep your friends close and your enemies closer.* Know where your opponent stands on the issue in question.
- *Maintain unity of command.* Weed out those who aren't falling into step to keep your colleagues in check.

- *Employ unexpected tactics such as deception, speed, audacity, and creativity.* Work quickly, and don't be shy.
- *Maintain secrecy until it is too late for your opponent to react.* The element of surprise can be your greatest asset. Don't advertise your strategy; keep it under wraps.
- *Keep your plans simple.* Forget the frills and do only as much as is needed to accomplish the task; keep your battle plans focused and direct.
- *Choose a flexible strategy so you can adapt to changing conditions.*
- *Keep a positive morale even in the face of setbacks.* Don't run at the first sign of opposition; perseverance sometimes pays dividends.
- *Maintain momentum until success is accomplished and acknowledged.*

Need to draw up battle plans? *Write them down.* It may sound a little nerdy, but I swear it works. I encourage all of my aspiring Amazons to script or storyboard what they are going to say and do, whether it's an appointment with a boss to discuss performance issues, or a presentation of a new idea to a client. Even football coaches diagram their plays, so don't feel weird about it. You have something you want to accomplish, and you need to stay on point. Write down what you're going to say and practice it. If you are afraid to ask for a bonus or more vacation time, for example, write out your rationale, and be clear. Then rehearse, aloud or in your mind, before meeting with your supervisor. Being prepared is your best defense.

DISCIPLINE #3:
THE AMAZON RESETTLES PRISONERS OF WAR

After fighting for something at work, there are always bridges to mend and relationships to cultivate. If the aftermath of a decision is not handled properly, you will be left with infighting and strife. Keep the momentum going until your *end* is accomplished. A united front in your department can conquer much more than one riddled with dissent.

As Heidi, head of a national beverage company, said, "When I finally won the job of supervisor for the entire sales force, I had to smooth some ruffled feathers. There were other people who really wanted that job, and I didn't want dissension in the ranks."

She needed to maintain unity of command now that some of her former competitors became her direct reports. "I sat down with each person and involved them in developing my plans for the department. I gave them projects to work on, so they could share some of the responsibility, but still know who was in charge."

Good Amazons spend time restoring order and harmony after a huge shake-up. Dealing with resentment and dissatisfaction from top-down decisions is par for the course. If egos are bruised in the process, cooperation can be hard to come by. She has to reassure and resettle her colleagues, so that they can adjust to a new collective vision. By coalition building, you will be able to stand against any future enemies.

Lizzie, an investment banker, said, "After we decided to focus on different goals for the year, I had two direct reports who were constantly grumbling and complaining. They didn't like how competitive things had gotten, and spent a lot of time thinking about how good things were before the changes. After working with them to ease the transition, I moved one of them to another department and the other started working part-time, and eventually got another job. It made my team so much stronger without their bad attitudes."

You don't necessarily have to get rid of people if they aren't falling into step, but you might need to move them out of your department or into new job responsibilities if they are going to stay with the company. Doing this may maximize unity and minimize fallout.

As Douglas MacArthur said, "A general is just as good or as bad as the troops under his command make him." Building a team that shares the new goals and the new visions will ensure peace and achieve your objective. Some people can't adapt, and separating these people from the others who can conform is a good Amazon's job.

"After the publicity and marketing departments merged into one, I tried to give some of the employees, who seemed to be having trouble, a little time to adjust. I had to keep repeating the new procedures with many of the veteran publicists and marketing execs. I also had to sort out some turf battles," Kendra, vice president of a record label, told me.

With a structural change such as this, Kendra's main goal was to make sure that she could trust the newly formed department to do what she needed, when she needed it. Not only did she have to rebuild the machine, she had to make sure it was well-oiled and working properly. Instead of bickering about territory, they had to learn to use one another's resources.

After a month, Kendra assumed the role of the Amazon and issued an ultimatum: You either find a way to make this partnership work or we find other people who can learn to cooperate. Their differences eventually smoothed out, and they began to work more synergistically, something that was absent before Kendra put her foot down. Instead of just using one department to promote new products, they could use two—cross-promotional opportunities were abundant.

When it's time to deal with an employee who's not working out, you don't have be cruel, but don't shy away from being forthright and honest. Letting someone go for poor performance can be traumatic, so be prepared for any reaction. Try to limit the volatility of the situation. Will they walk out that very day and leave all their work in midair? Will they act out?

You don't have to be needlessly confrontational. You can lead them into a conversation similar to "I know you're not happy here" or "This doesn't seem to be a good fit for you or me," and then (unless they are disrupting everyday work for everyone) give them some time to figure it out. Not just two weeks, but maybe a month or so. Remain open to solutions or methods of working that might improve the situation if it's salvageable.

Jessica, the principal of a clothing company, just acquired some more established labels, and inherited some very talented, but stubborn designers, who balked at the new management structure. "I decided to spend some extra money and hire a coaching/consulting firm to deal with any issues that came from the acquisition," she said. "If they went through the program, and still had issues with my design team, we would tell them to move on and wish them luck. If the coaching sessions helped us meld all the employees together in the firm, then it was money well spent." Just keep in mind that building a united team is as important as knowing when to dismantle one.

RULE #3:
WIN THE PEACE, NOT JUST THE WAR

Forming strong alliances after a restructuring or reorganization can be a daunting task. Try some of these tips to gain loyalty, respect, and trust from your group:

- *Pay homage to the people who are going to make a difference.* Your goal is to build the strongest team possible, and you can't worry about everyone's feelings or making everyone happy in the process. Resettling the group means doing what's best for the company, not each individual.
- *Try to get with the program.* Rather than fight losing battles with employees who want to go back to the "old way," look for new mountains to climb to invigorate the team instead. "Anyone who gets nostalgic on a regular basis is in the wrong frame of mind. I want people focusing on the future," said Teresa, a software consultant.

- *Make sure everyone understands the general operating procedures.* Be clear about how the new management's objectives will work so that things go as smoothly as possible. "I held a company meeting to tell everyone what my vision was for the reorganized division. I went into a lot of detail about the steps I wanted to take to streamline cumbersome systems, and I took time to answer any questions. It's important that everybody's involved in the plan buy-in at the outset," said Rhonda, an executive in a telecommunications company.
- *Don't burn bridges or let your pride stand in the way of mending a ruptured business relationship—the fewer enemies you have, the better.* One Amazon, Ann, a mortgage broker, left a company because she was overworked and undervalued. To make sure there were no hard feelings when she scored a new job, she gave her old boss a client referral. "You never know when I may run into him again, or need to ask for a favor or advice."

THE DARK SIDE OF THE AMAZON

Be careful not to confuse the Amazon role with that of the Gladiatrix, whose aggressiveness, abrasiveness, and bullying ways are not the way to retain control of situations or people.

Acting out of anger or revenge is no way to get what you want. Challenging authority is one thing, but doing it in a condescending or offensive way, or with the wrong party, is another. Excessively antagonistic reactions don't win border clashes—astuteness and a measured course of action do. Thoughtful planning must replace knee-jerk responses to get ahead.

DOMMERCISE: Become a Devotee of the Martial Arts
Take a self-defense class. Try your hand at karate, judo, kung fu, boxing, or kickboxing.

Now that you've got your Amazon role for upcoming battles, let's look at the Nurse role so you'll have the skills to tend to the wounded when the dust settles.

CHAPTER SEVEN
ARCHETYPE FIVE: THE NURSE

WHAT'S YOUR THERAPEUTIC MIND-SET?

Find out if you are an instinctual caregiver by taking the quiz below. Take a look at the statements below and rate yourself between 1 and 10. The higher you rate yourself for each statement below, the more accurate each statement fits you. You . . .

1. keep cool when others blow their stack. _____
2. smooth out ruffled feathers when there are conflicts. _____
3. are sensitive to symptoms of distress and provide adequate comfort whenever possible. _____
4. respect boundaries. _____
5. inspire group support. _____

If most of your answers are below 6, you may not pay attention when colleagues are uneasy. If you're not a natural nurturer, this chapter will give you tips on how to become one. If you think you're a natural medic, you may still need some training.

To the Nurse, the workplace might sometimes seem like a unit from *M*A*S*H* or a psychiatric ward, where triage and interventions are performed regularly. Like the famous nurses, Florence Nightingale, Margaret Sanger, and Clara Barton, the Corporate Dominatrix Nurse is constantly assessing the mental states of others and the overall health of the team. Many women (I won't go as far as to say all) have a talent for providing "medical assistance" or "first aid" to others—they are natural diagnosticians who have an instinctive talent for figuring out what's ailing a department, company, or individual, and nursing them back to health.

GET IN A NURSE STATE OF MIND WITH HEALING POWER

Caring is the essence of nursing.
—Leninger

The Nurse is one of the favorite fantasies of S&M devotees. She allows her client to feel protected, safe, and cared for. The Corporate Dominatrices do the same in the Nurse role—her coworkers are reassured by her evenness and cool head in the face of chaos. She knows how to react in a productive, comforting way.

In the face of hectic, bureaucratic traffic, it helps to have the Nurse on hand to change perspectives. She's got a positive, calming influence as well as healing expertise to sooth ills. Crisis situations are quarantined when she helps quell anger, frustration, or emotional outbreaks with coworkers or supervisors. She works to prevent an epidemic of bad attitude.

The outsourcing of jobs can be like a virus, infecting productivity and the work atmosphere. Frustrated, unsettled employees can hinder workflow and tempt others to jump ship. With surgical precision the Nurse is a morale booster. She addresses disruptive forces or bruised egos by massaging them until they are no longer a threat to the overall tone of the office.

A healthy corporate atmosphere is a creative one, making the healing power of the Nurse essential for the wellness of a company. She chooses clinical care over conflict, humanity over adversity, and composure over stress. A natural team player, her actions and her manner speak volumes. By remedying entanglements with coworkers and supervisors within divisions or departments, the Nurse works to prevent any damaging behavior from spreading and contaminating the running of the organization.

DISCIPLINE #1:
THE NURSE HAS STEADY HANDS

Many times you can't control what's going on around you, but you can control your reaction to it; that's where the Nurse comes in. This angel in white keeps her composure during an emergency. The Nurse knows that surviving a tough situation is a lot more challenging if you don't stay focused. When a crisis hits and everyone else starts to dissolve into emotional distress, she keeps a level head. Her decisiveness is reflected in her soothing tones of voice, and reassuring body language.

The Nurse comes in handy when helping a colleague during a tough departmental transfer. By tackling the situation head-on and not encouraging the closed doors and whispering of the rumor mill, the Nurse keeps the gossip from spreading and disrupting the division's goals.

Downsizing is often one of the most disruptive changes in the workplace. One Nurse, Joanne, had to support her friends after they found out that layoffs were imminent in their company. One of them became very angry and lashed out at her boss; another felt betrayed and burst into tears when she found out she was on the list to get the ax. They were distraught and let their anxiety, frustration, and fear control their actions.

Instead of joining in the pity party, Joanne told them both to focus on getting the best severance package possible and to try to secure freelance gigs to sustain them until they got other jobs.

She convinced them that pissing off management wasn't a good strategy.

Bad things happen in life and in business. When everyone else has lost their judgment, use the Nurse's clear head in order to find the best prescription. She is skilled in delicate, intricate matters of importance, and is immediately responsive with a remedy in tough, tense situations.

RULE #1:
BE REACTIVE, NOT RADIOACTIVE

Instead of allowing a catastrophe to escalate, the Nurse uses a medicinal approach to neutralize hysteria and help coworkers or bosses move toward an antidote.

Even if you have a Nurse who is the calming influence at work—someone with whom you talk things out to get your bearings—it's a huge advantage to uncover your inner Nurse when you feel the panic escalating around you. The first step is to find a clinical approach so you can take control of the matter at hand. If you do know a quintessential Nurse, keep that person in mind, or ask yourself WWND—What Would the Nurse Do? Sure, she's the one who keeps the level head when things get crazy and the loose cannons start firing, but how, exactly, does she do it? Use this checklist when facing an emergency, crisis, or demanding situation:

- *Don't go to pieces!* Whereas some people might react to a tense or awkward situation with shrill tones and rash actions, the Nurse is even-tempered with a smooth, easy manner. She doesn't let her stress or nervousness show in her voice or gestures. If you're really anxious and your hands are shaking, keep them in your lap until you've gained control. Tracy, a stockbroker, said, "I try to remember that I don't want to say or do anything I'll regret the next day or the next week. No matter how bad the situation, I'm still responsible for my actions. My job gets nuts, and everyone avoids the people who act like maniacs." Drama is like a one-night stand—it's heady stuff when you experience it, but you must remember that you're going to have to deal with the situation the morning after, so be careful in the heat of the moment, and protect yourself.

- *Don't let your personal life bleed into business.* Maintaining your business persona is always a must. Everything rides on your professionalism and model behavior, especially when you are the face of your own company. When you work for yourself, there are boundaries that need to be built in. If you have an office at home, you've got to make sure you keep your home situation separate from your professional situation—even if the baby is crying in the background. Emily, an independent real estate agent, said, "If I get stressed-out because my kid is misbehaving, I try not to convey that emotion to a client who happens to call right after a tantrum." It sounds like common sense, but you'd be surprised how many people don't realize how important it is to keep a lid on your personal life.

- *Is it really life-or-death?* As cliché as it sounds, sometimes in the corporate world, we forget that it's only business and no one is going to die. Reminding yourself of that can save energy and stress, and allow you to use the role of the Nurse to assess the situation. When something goes wrong or mishaps occur, ask yourself, "In five years, will this be something I will look back at and laugh about?" Considering the long-term effects can help you step out of the moment and gain perspective.

• *Remember to take a time-out.* Give yourself a moment or two before you react or draw conclusions. When you are feeling overwhelmed, you may need a breath of fresh air. Next time something happens—from a shift in company structure to an explosive disagreement—take a walk around the block.

Everyone has their own method for staying grounded. Take a moment to put together a checklist of what you'll do when you find yourself in a crisis situation and your stress level is rising.

DISCIPLINE #2:
THE NURSE TAKES EVERYBODY'S TEMPERATURE

Along with keeping a steady frame of mind, the Nurse is always aware of the atmosphere around her. She senses when tempers are about to flare, feelings might be hurt, or jealousies are arising. She is conscious of what's going on at all times in case she needs to administer triage before a situation worsens. She has a built-in thermostat that notifies her when tension levels are escalating. As the Nurse, you're tuning in and asking questions like: Are people anxious? On edge? Disengaged?

As Ramona, office manager for a public relations firm, said, "We work as a team in my office, which is usually very, very hectic. We rely on one another. When I get to work in the morning, we all check in with one another. I always try to get a sense of what mood everyone's in. If someone's having a bad day, or is in a bad mood, you know not to confront them and pick up the slack for them, and hope they'll do the same for you."

Katrina, a sales executive, surveyed her work atmosphere and found that her boss was completely out of touch with what her colleagues did or how they felt. In monthly meetings, each rep would provide detailed updates while the boss usually cleaned out her in-box, half-heartedly listening. Eventually the meetings became a waste of time, and some people stopped attending and just sent written updates via e-mail. "Everyone was insulted, and there was very little motivation to actually do good work for her." Recognizing this climate made it easier for Katrina to try to fix the communication breakdown between her boss and coworkers.

In your training to be a Nurse, make sure that before you check the company mercury levels, you check your own. Regardless of how much you rely on the other members of your department, you should always know your stress level and emotional state. *The key to taking the temperature of your peers or supervisor is also knowing what your temperature is; it's essential to gauge your own state of mind first.*

Are you showing up at the office with a chip on your shoulder? Are you obsessing over things that happened yesterday and not focused on the task at hand? Are you tuned out? Are you crabby, nervous, or absentminded? Check out your mood so you can better assess what's going on with your colleagues.

One marketing associate, Tina, said, "When I went through my divorce, everyone at the office was very supportive, but looking back, I wasn't truly engaged in work. I was squeezing in phone calls with the lawyer or my ex between meetings, and would wear my emotions on my sleeve. Luckily I had an understanding boss, but she finally told me she was concerned that some clients didn't feel I was attentive. Now I try very hard to keep my personal issues from interfering with work. I try to leave personal stuff for after five or during lunch to make sure my mind is on work."

THE NURSE HAS A SUPPORTIVE BEDSIDE MANNER

As the corporate candy striper, the Nurse instinctively looks out for others. Being in tune with everyone else is a quality that, dare I say, many men don't necessarily feel comfortable exhibiting. As one report found, male MBA grads mistake communications or soft skills (people proficiency) as fluff, and just focus on specific technical skills.

A survey among female MBA grads found they leaned toward team building as opposed to male MBA grads, who were "more analytically driven [and] focus[ed] on success and independence."[11] The Nurse is interested in the care of the entire unit and lightens things up when they get too heavy.

11. Ronald Alsop, "Men Do Numbers, Women Do Strategy," *The Wall Street Journal*, 21 September 2005.

RULE #2:
TIME FOR THE PERFORMANCE CHECKUP

More than 90 percent of Fortune 500 companies employ 360-degree evaluations in order to assess and develop employee teamwork and productivity. This type of appraisal—feedback from colleagues, supervisors, and clients that is honest and anonymous—allows people to align how they are perceived by others with how they perceive themselves.

"I had a couple of surprises from the feedback I got in my 360-degree review—it was a little startling. Apparently I needed to improve on a few things, including clear, concise communication. A lot of times, I just assumed people knew what I needed them to do," said Phyllis, a development manager. Having others evaluate your performance can open your eyes to what's truly happening at work.

Just as in a 360-degree evaluation, the Nurse is open to opinions and suggestions from others. If there is a misunderstanding or professional altercation, she must address it in order to get back on track. By playing the Nurse and giving yourself regular 360 examinations, you will better understand how you are seen and how to adapt in order to get better results. In your mini checkups, ask yourself:

• Are you being avoided in the halls or welcomed into meetings and offices?
• Have you been noticing if your coworkers are happy, satisfied, and focused? Do you notice hushed voices when you pass by? Are your

colleagues having department lunches, mingling, and cracking jokes in meetings, or are people afraid to speak their minds?

- Is there dissension in the ranks? Is management criticized and are employees judged, or is there mutual admiration and cooperative efforts to work together?
- Are you putting the kibosh on bad morale or office rumors among your peers, or encouraging them to fester? Are you egging people on or sensing the need for damage control?
- Do you just put your head down and get your work finished, or do you take the time to walk into a colleague's office and ask how their day is going?

Put in some time at the water cooler to test the climate in your workplace. Feel things out and just listen. Take a moment to check in with employees to see what's on their mind. Choose someone with whom you don't talk to all that often. Are you really aware of the undercurrents in your office? We can always be a little more in touch. Take an extra ten minutes to talk to a colleague, and you may find you learn something that gives you more insight than a ten-minute game of online solitaire could ever do.

DISCIPLINE #3:
THE NURSE APPLIES FIRST AID AS NEEDED

Sometimes the Nurse just needs to give support when a coworker has lost their confidence. Jamie, a financial consultant, used the Nurse to help a colleague feel better about a complicated presentation that the audience didn't seem to understand. His analysis was apparently too much for them to absorb, and they wound up interrupting him throughout the slideshow. After the Q&A session, he came into Jamie's office looking very disappointed, and asked if his talk had been unclear or muddled.

Jamie saw that her colleague needed a shot of confidence. "I told him that it wasn't as bad as he thought, and he just needed more practice speaking in front of people." She also related a horror story about the first time she gave a major presentation—she had toilet paper sticking out of her pants and she forgot her notes. "He had a good laugh and felt better." After injecting some humor (a handy painkiller) to dull the embarrassment, she also offered to listen to him practice any upcoming presentations and give advice.

Being conscious of other people's psychological well-being is a talent we could all stand to nurture, especially among managers and supervisors.

The Nurse also knows how to patch up severed relationships. When two interior designers in a textile firm, who had always been close friends, began competing for what they thought might be a career-making client, their long-standing professional and personal friendship began to deteriorate. Communication between the two stopped, and both felt the other should apologize. Their boss, Stacy, came up with a plan to patch things up.

She sent each an invitation to dine with her on the same night at the same place, and then stood them up so they had to face each other. "I knew if they spent time together in a relaxed atmosphere, after they stopped laughing about what I had done, they would realize how silly the whole thing was," Stacy told me. The tactic worked, and the two shared the account, and the firm was one big (mostly) happy family again.

THE NURSE GIVES A SHOT IN THE ARM

As Nurse, you need to know how and when to give a dose of truth serum. While the Nurse is often the caretaker, sometimes she has to switch from soothing to being straightforward. The truth hurts, but, like peroxide on a wound, sometimes it is what is necessary to ward off an infection—especially when others want to play the victim rather than proactively help themselves out of a rut.

Cynthia, an executive financial advisor, had to do just that—tell it like it is—to a fellow associate, Bruce, who had the "I can do nothing wrong" bug. When people gave him constructive feedback, he claimed they were trying to do his job, and he lashed out at them. As Cynthia said, "He was always igniting some type of a fire I had to put out. He wigged out all of the time! It was completely disruptive."

Cynthia was usually the most kind, supportive supervisor in the company, but Bruce was in need of a stern reality check. When he flipped because she had advised him against going forward with a seemingly dead-end investment proposal, he reacted by suggesting she was jealous. That was the final straw. "I told him that he was always looking at everyone but not himself, and he played the injured party. If he didn't get his act together, he would lose the respect of everyone in the company. I did him a favor by being honest with him, even if it wasn't a pleasant experience." Apparently it sunk in, because after thinking it over, he apologized the next day and worked hard not to point fingers or act so obvious about his insecurity in the future.

Playing the Nurse can also work to your advantage when

dealing with your boss. "It's impossible to work in a department where the direct reports are resentful because they feel isolated from the boss. They stop communicating because they think they're not being heard," Katrina, a marketing manager, told me. I advised her to tell her supervisor what was really going on—that the department felt out of touch with her. When she did, her supervisor was stunned. Since the boss was obviously overwhelmed and too busy to chair staff meetings, Katrina suggested that she run them and just update her boss. By doing this she freed up her boss's time while also positioning herself for more responsibility. Eventually Katrina was promoted to associate marketing director, and continued to liaise between direct reports and her supervisor.

THE NURSE ADMINISTERS CORPORATE TLC

An expert at dealing with the fragility of the psychological aspects of the workplace, the Nurse helps make tough situations bearable by prescribing "natural cures" and corporate tender, loving care.

While certain situations may fester with blunt, aggressive behavior, the Nurse knows how and when to use a softer, more soothing style. Emily, a music agent, had to use the Nurse role after she reprimanded an artist for crossing boundaries. The client badgered her constantly on her cell and was unreasonably high maintenance. "I was fed up because he called my cell at all hours." Emily found herself putting out fires all the time, even on holidays. She tried a firm approach, and in an attempt to set limits, told him not to call her on weekends. Setting these boundaries apparently hurt the client's feelings.

When her straightforward approach didn't work, she soothed

the client by telling him how important this project was to her and how she was dedicated to it wholeheartedly. Emily had learned her lesson; in the future she'd take a more delicate tactic with this client. As for those annoying calls during brunch and dinners—she just recognized his phone number and let it go to voice mail. If it was urgent, she responded. If not, she let it wait.

For those colleagues whose feathers are ruffled easily, the Nurse can heal a wounded ego with delicate precision. She fixes relationships and repairs potential misunderstandings to business that might jeopardize an important venture. "Sometimes it's easier just to coddle a client than to react the way you feel," said one mortgage consultant, Lydia.

Bessie, a divorce attorney, had an edgy client who always had a chip on his shoulder. When he got incensed one day about a bad turn in his divorce negotiations, he began taking it out on her. Instead of getting defensive, she reminded herself he was in the middle of an emotionally draining divorce and just wanted to feel taken care of. "I told him that I was sorry for his disappointment, and that he was in good hands and had nothing to worry about. I then added that I had just won him joint custody of his kids in the divorce negotiations. Needless to say, he felt a lot better." Her skills as a Nurse showed through her empathetic responses and patience—it also helped win her slews of referrals.

One human resources director, Marge, with a history of social services, said, "I tell my department that sometimes you just have to listen to someone's story or complaints, and the best medicine is to let them feel they have been heard."

RULE #3:
TAKE AN ASPIRIN AND
CALL ME IN THE MORNING

When you're trying to administer corporate TLC to the wounded ego, the functionally paranoid, or the tantrum prone, remember these tips:

- *Try to avoid a group confrontation and deal with the source of the infection.* By isolating the cause of an inflamed encounter and addressing the individuals involved in private, the Nurse uses tactfulness and instills trust.
- *Establish intake procedures.* When someone is unhappy because they don't feel they're getting respect, get the history behind the issue. Convey that you understand their concerns.
- *Make sure you're not patronizing them.* The last thing you want to do is make a coworker feel unimportant. Remember the saying from the movie *Jerry Maguire*, "Help me help you." Make sure you're alleviating a given situation instead of aggravating it with a condescending attitude.
- *Listen first, offer solutions later.* Try to break suggestions down into *realistic* and *unrealistic* bites to determine what is possible and impossible. Managing expectations is tricky business.
- *Don't assume that the answer to a request will always be yes.* We all need to recognize that we won't always have a happy ending. It's very likely there will be disappointments at work. The world

of business is not always fair and just, so be prepared for ups and downs.

- *Have an external advisor and work through challenges without taking opinion polls.* Blowing things out of proportion by asking for input from the entire department will only make matters worse. Although you may want to get validation from your peers, you need to work through some problems outside the walls of your office.

What's happening in your neck of the woods? Take some time to check out the scene and find a way to instill some positive energy into your workplace:

- Is there a relationship in need of repair? Take the high road. Maybe the person feels threatened by you, or needs your help.
- Is there someone in the department who has the antisocial virus and alienates colleagues? Don't be afraid to say so, even if it hurts their feelings. It could potentially hurt them more if they are never told.
- Is there a new employee who feels like an outcast? Stage an intervention and invite him out for drinks after work.
- Is someone acting out to try to get attention? Sometimes people just want to get their fifteen minutes of fame. Give them confidence with a kind word of encouragement.

THE DARK SIDE OF THE NURSE

Codependency is a no-no. Trying to revive a terminal situation at work can be exhausting and a waste of time, and sometimes you run the risk of losing your own work focus in the shuffle. The dark side of the Nurse's role is that she might forget to take care of herself as she tends to others. Even though tending to the overall well-being of your workplace is necessary, it should be done in moderation. Knowing when to be selfless and when to put your focus back on your own business is part of the finesse of a good Nurse. As one chief executive officer told me, "Team health is important, and so is being a good worker, but in the end, you look out for you." Sometimes you just do not resuscitate.

DOMMERCISE: Always Be Prepared

Are you ready for all contingencies? Make sure you've got some aspirin, Advil, or Band-Aids in your desk drawer. Think of increasing your ministering skills by taking a first-aid class or learning CPR.

Next up, the Schoolgirl. Put on your knee-high socks and your plaid skirt, and get ready to study up on how to get an A every time.

CHAPTER EIGHT
ARCHETYPE SIX: THE SCHOOLGIRL

WHAT'S YOUR SCHOLASTIC MIND-SET?

Let's find out if you are a teacher's pet. Take a look at the statements below, and rate yourself between 1 and 10. The higher you rate yourself for each statement below, the more accurate each statement describes you. You . . .

1. balance productivity with popularity. _____
2. give authority the respect it earns and play along with someone else's agenda when it's in your best interest. _____
3. use reliability and dependability to build your reputation and make yourself indispensable. _____

4. realize that being well behaved has its merits and "manipulation" is not a dirty word. _____

5. use comedy as a strategy. _____

If most of your answers are below 6, you need to be reminded why Schoolgirls do so well in class. This chapter will jog your memory. If you think you're an A student, you may still need some private corporate tutoring.

Dorothy from *The Wizard of Oz* is the poster child for the Schoolgirl role. Feisty and precocious, the Schoolgirl is in a seemingly submissive role—she borrows power to get ahead. The Corporate Dominatrix relies on the power of those in higher positions when in the Schoolgirl role, just as Dorothy drew on the power of the Wicked Witch of the East's ruby slippers and the help of the Tin Man, the Scarecrow, and the Cowardly Lion.

The Schoolgirl is disarmingly strong. Rather than push her weight around, she's not afraid to let others take control of the wheel while she remains a subtle backseat driver. She shares in the tasks at hand. She asks for advice when she needs it. And she knows how to shore up those around her when they are feeling put out or out of sorts. This Schoolgirl may seem naïve, but she acts submissive to gain the upper hand. Her ability to work with inflated or delicate egos without being an overt toadie is her gift.

GET IN A SCHOOLGIRL STATE OF MIND
WITH BORROWED POWER

*It is, all in all, a historic error to believe that the master
makes the school; the students make it!*
—Robert Musil

The Schoolgirl draws on her inner child, repressed girlishness, and lessons from the classroom for her power. Unlike all other roles of the Corporate Dominatrix, she is strategically submissive to authority or imperceptively dominant. She understands how to balance drive with deference. In her complaisance, she may outwardly honor authority or have an ingratiating regard for management. She may seem nonthreatening and cheerful (and she may be!), but her obedience is her power, and it can propel her agenda under certain circumstances. Her borrowed power from key players is unobtrusive, merely tucked away out of sight, allowing others to feel comfortable, at ease, and good about themselves.

Just as a young child has to ask others to hand them the out-of-reach cookie jar, so do people in subordinate positions need to borrow power and ask for help from senior executives. Association power helps you gain face time and a good foothold by your proximity and access to an influential person.

THE SCHOOL OF HARD KNOCKS

Every person has a dominant and submissive side, even if it doesn't seem completely obvious at first. Almost all mistresses are dominant at heart, and don't particularly care to play the submissive role with clients. Neither do their Corporate Dominatrix cousins, but it's all part of the job sometimes, right? Broadening her repertoire, she can switch to a submissive role, even if, in the end, she tops from the bottom. Even with the most dominant personalities, there is always a need for them to be, on some level, submissive to someone.

The Schoolgirl is an essential role for the Corporate Dominatrix's success under certain conditions. Almost everyone has to be submissive to authority now and then; even if you're at the top, you may have clients or stockholders to answer to. A tax lawyer, Patricia, admitted, "I'm the one who is usually the most assertive in meetings, and I generally run the show, and tell people what to do. At home, I'm the submissive one in my relationship. I can't always be dominant, and sometimes I need a balance." If you're always dominant at work, and are sometimes submissive out of the workplace, switch and allow the Schoolgirl to make an appearance at work a little more often.

THERE CAN BE STRENGTH IN SUBMISSION TO THE CORPORATE HIERARCHY

Just because you're submissive to the "bureaucratic system," doesn't mean you're a wimp! The key is making sure that "submission" doesn't suggest you are subservient or allow others to step on you. As one S&M expert said about a "good submissive," this is someone who "who respects herself [and] someone who doesn't want . . . abuse."[12]

---

12. Phillip Miller and Molly Devon, *Screw the Roses, Send Me the Thorns: The Romance and Sexual Sorcery of Sadomasochism* (Fairfield, CT: Mystic Rose Books, 1995), 41–42.

Just because you're compliant doesn't mean you suffer fools easily or don't respect yourself. Remember this and you will always be a successful Corporate Dominatrix: You are always in charge, regardless of whether you are playing a submissive or dominant role. The Schoolgirl eludes the submissive stereotypes, striking a delicate balance: She is obedient yet mischievous, acquiescent yet engaged and motivated, and even though she is coy, she is forthright and honest.

SUGAR-'N'-SPICE AND EVERYTHING NICE

It's no surprise that researchers find girls tend to do better in school. More so than the corporate world, schools primarily reward obedience rather than risk-taking and rebellion. A journalist, Martha Brockenbrough, called these obedient female profiles sugar-'n'-spice personalities or teacher's pets, commenting on the necessity of conformity: "Obedience helps schools run more calmly, and risk-taking helps businesses earn more money. Both types of personalities exist, and both are necessary."

As discussed earlier, researchers found that dominant women are viewed more negatively than dominant men, indicating that behavior inconsistent with gender roles is not well-received. The study also found that women who act according to their specific gender roles are viewed as more competent than women who do not. The trick to success is being able to make strides managerially while still remaining feminine, and having the skills to sprinkle a little sugar-'n'-spice around when necessary.

In certain scenarios, like a performance review or a conference, being argumentative or confrontational won't get you very far. Sometimes you need to be obedient to survive. Call in the Schoolgirl and she'll lead you out of your dominant role (Goddess, Queen, Governess, Amazon, or Nurse) into one that will better fit the situation. This is not a role you ever want to stay in for an extended amount of time, but one you want to do on demand.

DISCIPLINE #1:
THE SCHOOLGIRL TOPS FROM THE BOTTOM AND BOTTOMS FROM THE TOP

One of the most conflicted and complicated roles, the Schoolgirl has an agenda even when she seems to be going along with the program. This power play is often called "topping from the bottom" and "bottoming from the top." "Top" is used for the dominant role and "bottom" is the word used for the submissive role. When someone is topping from the bottom, it means that even though they appear subordinate on the surface, they are really calling the shots and directing the action. Bottoming from the top allows you to flip the dynamic. You are in a senior position, but defer your power and let others take charge. Your behavior belies your title.

Donna, an executive secretary at a prestigious law firm, began borrowing power in the Schoolgirl role when she began simplifying legal letters to clients on behalf of her boss, based on her close relationships with them.

Instead of just keyboarding his dictation, she would fashion his correspondence in an approachable way without jeopardizing legal content. Rather than asking permission, she pursued her mission: to make sure her boss looked good. When a client called saying that he appreciated the letter and the way everything was easily explained in layman's terms, her boss found out and he was very appreciative. Word got out, and other secretaries asked for Donna's tricks of the trade. "It was as if I was the expert on massaging legal correspondence from that point on."

This lady knows how to top from the bottom, and she looks good as a result. She worked in an unobtrusive, subtle way to build her boss's image. She doesn't mind if others get the credit, because it will eventually come back to her. By borrowing power from the attorney, she felt comfortable because she knew how to represent her boss in writing. Making yourself invaluable to your supervisor and the company as a whole is one way to guarantee security.

Proactivity, cleverness, and adaptability help no matter how small the task or how "beneath" you it might be. Setting aside feelings of entitlement can also put you in subtle yet powerful control of situations with people above you . . . or below you.

Molly is a senior account executive under the executive vice president at a pharmaceutical company. Her boss would often give her things to do, such as processing client paperwork or booking conference rooms for meetings—in other words, ask her to "bottom from the top." When someone is bottoming from the top, she performs tasks that are beneath her position when there is a cost benefit attached. Molly would occasionally play the Schoolgirl and deal with small requests that came her way instead of saying, "Why don't we just have your secretary take care of that?" It gave her the opportunity to liaise with the assistant for the chief executive officer, who became very fond of her and gave glowing reports to *her* boss. Soon, the chief executive officer was requesting account information from Molly directly. She grew increasingly more involved in the details that dictated some of the most successful projects, and the executive vice president trusted her completely. *No matter what the position, even if you're the president, sometimes you need to be a good Schoolgirl.*

RULE #1:
IT'S NOT A BOTHER, IT'S A BARTER

Next time there's a task that's up for grabs for the big kahuna, don't immediately think, "That's so beneath me, and I'm way too busy." Instead consider whether or not bottoming from the top might help you down the line. Ask yourself a few questions:

• Would this task give you more kudos in a supervisor's eyes?
• Would this give you a chance to slip some of your own ideas into the mix?
• Would this give you more access to people and situations that might strategically help you in the long run?

If the answer to any of these questions is yes, see if you can make time to do it.

DISCIPLINE #2:
THE SCHOOLGIRL DISARMS WITH CHARM

The Schoolgirl is anything but innocent, but through her curiosity and playfulness, she knows how to act the part. In the office it's easy to forget that you don't have to always know everything all the time, and apprenticeships never really end. We're always able to learn more if we take advantage of other people's knowledge.

The Schoolgirl coaxes people out of their competitive, hardnosed business world by being inquisitive and self-effacing. When someone lets their guard down, it's a lot easier to gain their support and slip into a mutually advantageous working relationship.

ASK, DON'T TELL—BE NONCONFRONTATIONAL

When you're delegating, critiquing, or instructing someone in a touchy situation, it helps to put the suggestion in the form of a question. The Schoolgirl knows how to plant an idea without being intimidating, annoying, or overly demanding.

Here are some examples:

- Instead of saying, "This ad is all wrong," you might recommend, "Why don't you try one or two other directions for the ad and let's compare them?"
- Instead of saying, "The concept for the presentation is not what

we discussed," you might try, "Did you have any other ideas for the presentation? I'd like to see a list of all the suggestions we discussed as well as other recommendations."

The Schoolgirl is sensitive to "musterbation," a term coined by Dr. Albert Ellis. It describes the tendency to think something "must" occur or "must" be done—a common feeling in a 24/7 workplace. You can only do the best you can in the time you have. Also be on the lookout for shoulda-woulda-coulda thinking. Don't second-guess yourself!

Using the Schoolgirl can produce a less imposing and more amiable style. In this role you can manage the dynamic between you and your coworkers and remove any competitiveness that might be a turnoff.

The Schoolgirl is sharp and knowing. She's astute and can occasionally speak truth to power, yet no one finds her insubordinate. As with the saying "Out of the mouths of babes come pearls," she does not offend, insult, or threaten with her tone of voice or her body language. Letting down your know-it-all guard, and being vulnerable as the Schoolgirl can do a couple of things:

1. *You cease to be a threat when you are asking for someone's help, advice, or support.* The simple inflection in your voice can put others at ease. We're advised to appear buttoned-up so often, that sometimes we forget there might be an advantage to acting the opposite way. Go easy on yourself every once in a while; don't be afraid to admit what you don't know. You are putting people in the position of being knowledgeable when you seek advice. Everyone loves to be

an expert about something; it's no secret that most people love to talk about themselves and what they know. So let them.

The Schoolgirl is eager to absorb other people's expertise on a need-to-know basis. You want to be a sponge and learn as much as you can in order to broaden your network and skill set.

As one Schoolgirl, Anna, said, "Admitting you don't know how to do something is about being secure in your ego. My pride doesn't necessarily get in the way of my ambition—I know I'm good at my job. People really appreciate it when you're honest and don't try to put up a false front about knowing something you might not. . . . I don't mind saying 'I don't understand,' or 'I don't know.'"

I had a supervisor who used this to her advantage all the time—she was never afraid to say that she didn't understand something. All of the employees respected that about her; she didn't sit on her high horse, and became less like the distant Queen and more like an approachable Schoolgirl.

One online marketing manager, Amy, was having a problem with a hard-to-handle boss who always picked over everything she did. And whenever she tried to explain herself he would get even more angry. Rather than spinning her wheels with explanations when he was giving her a hard time, she needed to ask for his instruction and how he liked particular things done—the change of focus was productive; he enjoyed sharing his business know-how and started to cut her some slack.

2. *Disarm; don't take up arms unnecessarily.* Drop aggressive behavior that might inspire any kind of hostility or fear. By drawing out your colleagues and getting them to open up, you may learn some things you didn't know about them. When people start talking about themselves, you tend to learn some very interesting things about their nature.

Alicia, a stockbroker, had a reputation as being a prig. Some of her coworkers felt she was a little preachy and tended to steamroll people when she wanted to make a point. As a result, people's eyes would glaze over when she would begin to talk and they stopped asking for her opinion about things; she even got bumped from meetings. Her overbearing, opinionated image needed a little patching up. After all, if you're all-knowing, you're not growing. Instead of bludgeoning people with her ideas every chance she got, she need to play the Schoolgirl every once in a while.

After a trip to charm school, Alicia became more comfortable in the Schoolgirl role. When she felt the impulse to interrupt someone, she paced herself and tried to listen and respect her audience. When she paid attention or asked people questions about themselves (instead of butting in with her own stories), she learned some valuable lessons about how she could better get along with her coworkers. "I noticed a big difference in the way people were treating me. They were more cordial in general. After a while, they paid attention to my ideas, not my behavior." Alicia's winning demeanor did wonders when she wanted to make people feel more at ease.

RECESS: PLAYTIME HELPS YOUR GAME TIME

The Schoolgirl knows how to play and make things a little more fun for everyone. A sense of humor can help you get through a tough day at work, but it can also remind others to have a laugh and not take things so seriously.

Sue, a booking agent, said, "I had a great relationship with my boss. I also knew she could lose her temper really easily. She even asked me to kick her under the conference table if she got carried away in meetings." Sue became the Schoolgirl with her boss in these situations, whereas everyone else would be subject to her dominating, fiery temper tantrums. Sue was able to kid with her and say things like "You might see that outburst on your report card" after hearing about one of her boss's explosions. She became her boss's confidant instead of her scapegoat. Coaxing people with your playfulness can help you wiggle out of misunderstandings or tight spots.

RULE #2:
TAP INTO YOUR INNER CHILD

When writing *Rejuvenile: Kickball, Cartoons, Cupcakes, and the Reinvention of the American Grown-up*, Christopher Noxon found more and more adults are seeking out ways of "maintaining wonder, trust, and silliness" to balance their adult responsibilities. It's not a bad idea for you to do the same when you want to disarm someone at work, or even give yourself a break from the daily professional pressures.

By returning to a more naïve sense of self that doesn't revolve around high-powered superiority complexes, you can rediscover and explore another aspect of your personality that has more to do with lighthearted banter, impishness, and amusement.

To help you get into your little girl frame of mind, answer the following questions:

- Do you make time to notice everything around you the way you did as a kid?
- What was your favorite game as a child?
- Was there something in particular you did to get your way with adults?
- What secrets did you keep and when did you decide to share them?

Now, think about your answers and go over them. Use these questions to conjure some memories that can help you remember how it was to be younger—less concerned about daily stresses and more carefree. Were you braver about saying what you thought? Were you smart-alecky, sassy, or cheeky? If so, bring that little lady to life. If not, now's your chance to liven up that little-girl personality.

DISCIPLINE #3:
THE SCHOOLGIRL FLATTERS
THROUGH IMITATION

Flattery can come in many shapes and sizes. There's the most obvious kind—like direct compliments—and then there is the one that can help you learn and grow: imitation and emulation. By mirroring people around you, you can get the lay of the land, the lingo, the politics, and the procedures. While there's a time and a place to assume your own identity, patterning yourself after successful business gurus or a respected colleague can be useful as you win friends and influence people.

By imitation, I don't mean you should become a clone of your managers or coworkers. The Schoolgirl gets the lowdown from people who are in the know, and she absorbs the larger lessons they have to teach her into her repertoire. By doing this, she can glean some nuggets from their experience and endear herself to them. Here are some tips to the art of imitation:

LISTEN AND LEARN
Pay attention to what supervisors and colleagues who are knowledgeable have to say—not just the concept but the actual language. Grab on to that jargon and use it. That doesn't mean that you always need to say whatever they say word for word; you can make it your own.

In business, buzzwords abound. You might notice seasoned

professionals use words such as "synergy," "decentralization," "barriers to entry," "deliverables," "market leader," or "mind share," for example. Using particular expressions in the right context can show you know your stuff. Take some time to listen carefully and do some research on the phrases in your particular field. If you hear a word you don't understand, look it up. Overuse or misuse of words or clichés can produce a very undesirable affect, so be careful and study up!

Beyond jargon, management might be fixated on particular benchmarks. One client, Ginny, an attorney, noticed that the partners were always reiterating the goal for their division—"national prominence." This was a phrase she heard over and over. She took to using it when pitching to clients and even in the hiring process—would this candidate help bring her law firm "national prominence"? Just as kids imitate their parents (sometimes for better or worse), you can do the same thing.

Becky, an office manager for a real estate company, was transitioning into working as an actual agent. Becky was nervous because though she was experienced in the real estate field, she never sold homes or showed properties. I advised her to use the strengths of the Schoolgirl by asking if she could go on sales calls or work on open houses with a more experienced agent. Shadowing another agent worked and she eventually incorporated what she learned into her own dealings with potential clients. She also asked to be included in long-term strategy meetings, when her boss reviewed the hot new neighborhoods under development in the city. When describing her agency's approach to clients, she rehashed the concepts she had learned from her coworkers, and everyone was impressed with her adaptability. Her boss noticed, and he took her under his wing to groom her while she worked toward getting her real estate license.

DO YOUR HOMEWORK

You may find yourself in the position of the Schoolgirl if you've been given some type of new responsibility or inherit projects from coworkers. Even if it's not rocket science, better yourself by playing the student every once in a while. Learning more about whatever you're doing will keep you on the cutting edge of trends, a place the Corporate Dominatrix always likes to be.

Make a habit of reading up on and seeking out the most successful business people in your industry and learn from them. Become an observer of impressive people; everyone has something to teach you. By following seasoned advice, you can enhance your standing at meetings, conferences, or presentations.

Seek information in every available medium—books, DVDs, CDs, the Internet—it will help shape your career goals and sharpen your expertise. Subscribe to business magazines, trade newsletters, or just do some inquisitive Googling. This truth always stands: Knowledge is powerful. Use what you learn so you don't forget it— you'll retain the concepts a lot longer if you apply them right away.

One client, Roxy, sold advertising space for a small magazine. She had never done the ad contracts before, but when the department lost an assistant, her boss wanted her to process the paperwork herself. The task proved daunting. "I don't want to go into my boss's office every ten minutes with a question, and even worse, I don't want to screw up a contract!" she lamented. I told her to do her homework: Not only could she use the library and the Internet, but she could also try taking a class in magazine advertising. In addition, I recommended she join a magazine trade organization and try to get in touch with someone who had been doing ad sales. She did, and asked an active member to lunch. He loved talking about all the tricks of the trade—and Roxy took extensive notes. Before long, she got the contract part of her job down pat.

Doing your homework makes you *feel* prepared and more confident. When I was managing a department for the first time, I read a ton of books on management, particularly by Peter Drucker and Tom Peters. I also observed really good managers in action. And upon receiving a compliment from them, I would admit, "I got that from you" or "You taught me everything I know."

By actively using the concepts you learn, you can bring your knowledge to fruition and your career to its highest potential.

BECOME A TECHIE

One client, Pat, an assistant to the owner of a sportswear company, shared that her boss doesn't know how to check e-mail. "I print out all his e-mails and it delays his ability to respond. I'm working on raising his comfort level and confidence on the computer so he can check e-mail himself," says Pat. "I always tell him how quickly he picks things up." Whether you're at the top or not, keep yourself sharp by always learning new technologies or risk becoming a dinosaur. With emerging innovations, information networks, and interactive models—whether that means operating a new software program, a newfangled electronic gadget, or videoconferencing equipment—there is always a new innovation, and you don't want to be left in the dust.

BAIT AND SWITCH

Now on to the more obvious type of flattery. Compliments add an element of admiration and approval. Don't get carried away and say anything untrue for your own gain, but you can certainly use praise to acknowledge the work of colleagues and put yourself into their good graces.

Stroking egos with a compliment is a good way to take the attention off something you're avoiding or don't want to address. The benefit is twofold: You change the subject and you make the person feel great. For example, if you know someone's headed to your office to bring up a mistake you've made, a deadline you've missed, or an issue you're not ready to address, as the person rushes into your office, look up and say, "Wow, nice shirt!" or "Did you get a haircut? The style suits you." Result: You've bought some time and you're on their good side.

MAKE SURE SUPERIORS FEEL SUPERIOR

When holding influencers in high regard, remember that they are also human and prone to the same insecurities as the rest of us. You want to strike a balance by appearing capable and confident and also pay your respects to the King or Queen of their domain.

One client, Kenda, a director of development in a production company, was on a roll with acquiring new clients. Everything seemed to be going great, but she couldn't figure out why her boss was not inviting her to key meetings and behaving aloof. She was exasperated. "I thought we had a solid relationship, but in the past few months, he has been harder and harder to communicate with." After figuring out what had changed in recent months—her client list had grown almost as large as his—she understood that she needed to make him feel more secure and less threatened by her. Every chance she got, especially in meetings, she began giving him credit for mentoring her. She also asked his advice on how to juggle so many projects. Ultimately he started feeling better about things and eventually his department was recognized as a top-revenue performer, which was a big win for everyone.

STROKING NEUTRALIZES ENVY AND JEALOUSY IN COWORKERS

Invalidate contentious behavior by killing the competition with kindness; recognize their work and talents, and play the sweet Schoolgirl. This can be a lot more effective than overreacting or blowing a gasket. Bide your time, though, since you can make your point when they *least* expect it.

Kathleen, a finance specialist, said, "There was one woman who seemed to shoot zingos in my direction now and then. Every time I felt things getting tense, I would pat her on the back and she would get off mine. I even asked her advice on a few proposals, telling her, 'You're an expert on this subject,' and I could tell it made her feel less threatened." The way to deal with "mean" girls or "bad" boys is to confuse them by being courteous and respectful.

This applies to clients too. Telling them that you're thrilled to be working with them on a regular basis is a good practice. Don't just do it in the beginning; remind them throughout the relationship that you're happy they're with you and make them feel special and valued.

RULE #3:
AUDITION FOR THE UNDERSTUDY

Just as the Schoolgirl learns her lessons when brushing up on her job skills, she displays a healthy interest in other people's careers or expertise. Familiarizing yourself with the supporting cast is important for a Corporate Dominatrix. The more you know about what other people do, the more you're able to help those in particular positions if necessary. It will also give you experience if you want to transfer to another area. You will gain a better understanding of the big picture and how your company operates as a whole.

Throughout my career, I tried to pick up additional skills from colleagues in other parts of the company. It makes sense that employees who fare the best in the long run are the people who understand the workings of the other cogs in the machine.

Sit down with someone in a different department that you would like to understand better. You might discover something you didn't know, which may ultimately help you at your job or give you background for a career move. Ask questions, be inquisitive, and take the role of an apprentice. A sales representative may have a lot to learn from an associate in the advertising group with a whole different set of skills.

THE DARK SIDE OF THE SCHOOLGIRL

Overplaying this or any role can potentially be damaging for your career advancement. As one executive said, "I played the Schoolgirl with my boss through the years. Even though he adored me, he passed me over for a promotion that I had been waiting for. He didn't see me as a contender because I was too much of a helpmate and I didn't toot my own horn enough. I guess he didn't think I was independent enough." Maybe that's what happened, or she knew how to make him feel so good about himself that he didn't want to let her go. The moral of this story: You don't want people to hold you back just because you're allowing them to stand tall.

DOMMERCISE: Educate Yourself

Stay ahead of the curve with distance learning courses online (the University of Phoenix is popular) and adult education classes. Subscriptions to trade journals, newsletters, and blogs will also keep you in the know and up-to-date on your industry.

Well, you've met all the Corporate Dominatrix sisters—the Goddess, the Queen, the Governess, the Amazon, the Nurse, and the Schoolgirl—it's time to take them to the office!

CHAPTER NINE
THE CORPORATE DOMINATRIX GOES TO WORK
(AND WORKS IT)

Playing the mistress can help you in all areas of your life because it helps you take control and stay in control. She has a firm grip on the reins of her world and makes the rules in her environment. Now picture yourself being able to consciously direct this aura to encompass people around you. It will cloak you in mystery, and who doesn't love a good mystery?
—Claudia Varrin,
author of *The Art of Sensual Female Dominance*

Now that you have the six mistress archetypes at your disposal, as well as the types of power they wield, learning when to use each of these will make the Corporate Dominatrix in you unstoppable. By viewing your coworkers as tops, bottoms, and switchables, you will instinctively know how best to manage them—and yourself.

You may see your boss as more than just a highly dominant supervisor; she might be an Amazon or Queen. Or your colleague might be more than just an organizational taskmaster; now you know her as a Governess. Switching from your core work persona (or defining self) to another Corporate Dominatrix archetype will give you the particular power you need to "win friends and influence people" in the workplace.

You have X-ray vision that will help you see each office encounter from a new perspective. Once you start looking at people in the context of the sadomasochistic workplace, you'll be able to use role-play to effectively move through the corporate hierarchy. "After reviewing the archetypes, I realized that my associate is a classic Amazon with a dark side, and I use the Schoolgirl or the Nurse to get along with her," said Suzanne, a television producer. "Once I saw my colleagues in dominant and submissive terms, I felt like I had the upper hand, and understood them in a profound, new way."

When I spent time with professional dominatrices, I noticed they could nail someone's MO (or modus operandi) from a mile away. One dominatrix would just point and rattle off the labels "submissive" and "dominant" as we walked down the street! Her antenna was so tuned in to body language and facial expressions that she knew immediately what everyone's power vibe was. After some practice, you too will be able to read people with the same speed and accuracy. As Robin Shamburg writes when she left her dominatrix days behind her in *Mistress Ruby Ties It All Together*, "Fortunately . . . one thing I hadn't yet lost was my skewed sensibility, what I like to call the 'Lens of Leather.' No matter where I looked, I saw everything as an exchange of power, or the playing of a role, or as a negotiation between people—for good or for bad. The dungeon just happened to be a very extreme version of how people lived every day. As above, so below—it seemed like even the Holy Bible was acquainted with the S&M underworld."

PLAYING THE HAND YOU'RE DEALT

These mistress roles are now yours, for work and for play. Every time you enter into an interaction with someone else, imagine you're playing a game of poker. You may be dealing with Queens, Governesses, or Schoolgirls, and you've got to choose a Corporate Dominatrix archetype that can work with that particular person or accommodate that particular situation. Just like professional poker players, when you assume roles at work, make sure your intentions are kept under wraps and place your bets carefully.

You've got the control, so know when to hold and when to fold. Instead of relying solely on the "suits" or "types" you've been dealt (a boss who always makes you feel like a Schoolgirl, or a colleague who always puts you in the position of Governess), as the Corporate Dominatrix, you've got a full house of sisters in a stacked deck who are at your beck and call when you need them. Choose your role consciously and don't allow others to do it for you.

THE CORPORATE THEATER OF THE ABSURD

Now that you are well versed in the different roles you can play, you're ready to apply them in your day-to-day activities. The art of the mistress lies in understanding the mind-set and methodology of those roles and using them wisely. As you enter the theater of the workplace (that we won't hesitate to call *absurd*), let me outline the three stages of becoming the Corporate Dominatrix.

STAGE #1:
ESTABLISH YOUR DEFINING ROLE

The roles you automatically identify with, as discussed in Chapter Two, are your defining roles. Everyone has an instinctive mode of operation, a natural or core state. I've had friends say, "Oh yeah! I'm an Amazon" or "I was born a Governess!" Some women may even feel they're split between two of the archetypes, in which case they have a primary or defining role as well as a secondary role. That's fine, too; just don't get carried away with multiples!

There's an upside to playing your defining role in the workplace—you're probably really good at it, since you are intuitively attracted to the traits of that type. Once you've determined your defining role, the next step is to exercise control at all times over *when* and *how* it defines you. We immediately identify with one or two of these roles—that's the easy part. The challenge is to break out of your defining role, working against your impulse to default to a single archetype. If you're always a Queen, you've got to learn to try out some other types when necessary.

Beware of typecasting. The tricky thing about your defining role is that you have to make sure you don't get stuck allowing people to typecast you. As a Corporate Dominatrix, you want other people to be able to see beyond your defining roles. If you're most comfortable as an Amazon, you want others to be able to accept you as a Schoolgirl when the situation calls for it. Throw your colleagues off guard once in a while. Your goal in role-playing is to try on different roles and see how they fit. As a Corporate Dominatrix, you need room to grow. Just sticking to one role will stunt your career growth and encourage others to pigeonhole you.

Break out of the mold and shatter the stereotypes that might be surrounding your reputation. Like actors and actresses, you too want to experiment as you try different roles that may not immediately signal your "type." Hilary Swank, for example, played a transgendered teen, and then a boxer, and won Oscars for "serious" roles, as opposed to being typecast as an ingénue. As you confront the different daily situations, remember: The devoted Corporate Dominatrix is never satisfied with only the role she is expert in. She is always up for a challenge.

To get ahead, you've got to break out of your comfort zone, or how you normally act, and shift into a role that forces you to explore different parts of your personality and areas of skill.

Remember, comfort can be a cage, and if you develop your abilities in other roles, you will be free to take your career where you want it to go without limitations. Winning Oscars for your defining role is an easy shot, like repeating the same class you already got an A in.

The whole objective for the Corporate Dominatrix is to be in control of her image and attitude rather than allowing others to control them. The more inflexible you are in your roles, the more people you work with might typecast you. While it's difficult not to let your defining role dominate, you must practice other roles as circumstances arise. This will help you avoid traps, such as "She can't do that job; she's not aggressive enough" or "She can't work under that type of supervisor; she's too head strong." Be aware of your defining role; that's the first step to acknowledge whether you're subconsciously ruled by it.

STAGE #2:
ROLE TAKING—CHOOSING THE PART
YOU WANT TO PLAY

You've been playing roles your whole life; now you're just being more mindful of how you are using them in your career. Strategically and purposefully, applying your corporate "personalities" will give you more adaptability options when confronted with a variety of workplace scenarios. As the Corporate Dominatrix, you've got to be cognizant of the roles you are *taking*. This might seem very simple, but it is essential to alternating among these six sisters.

As Tian Dayton, PhD, author of *The Drama Within*, says, "Role taking or modeling is perhaps the most powerful form of teaching.... The role taking forms a brain template that is referred to again and again as familiar."[13] It's like riding a bike—once you get the hang of taking certain roles when you need them, it will feel old hat.

You might have a bulldog boss who requires you to play the Schoolgirl sometimes, even though you are at heart a Governess. Or, you may have wanted to play an Amazon to get a personal point across, but you stayed with your defining Nurse role too long (like a habit you couldn't break) and worked unselfishly for the benefit of the team.

Use your laser focus to access the circumstances and decisively choose which role to play. And don't underestimate the importance of rehearsing—practice makes perfect! The Corporate Dominatrix "acts in" when taking on the power of the role she's assuming. "Acting in" involves finding the appropriate role and absorbing its power. Depending on what comes up and when, she goes through her mental checklist, asking herself: Which type of power, and corresponding role, do I need now? Personal power (Goddess), position power (Queen), expert and reward powers (Governess), coercive power (Amazon), borrowed power (Schoolgirl), or healing power (Nurse)?

Essentially role taking is the act of making an informed decision as to how you *present yourself*. Choose the role, step into character, and act as though you own it.

13. Tian Dayton, *The Drama Within: Psychodrama and the Experiential Therapy* (Deerfield Beach, FL: Health Communications, 1994), 23.

STAGE #3:
ROLE-PLAYING—LIGHTS, CAMERA, ACTION

Now the real fun begins. When you role-play, you "act out" or explore the role through the unpredictable interactions with your colleagues. "The real point here is that playacting, being an actress, even if you are only playing the strong side of yourself, is part and parcel of domination," says Claudia Varrin, author of the *Art of Sensual Female Dominance*.

The Corporate Dominatrix is an illusionist and sometime opportunist. Your ability to role-play effectively will enhance your ability to dominate, even when you exhibit a submissive side. The Corporate Dominatrix knows that every chance to role-play (or act out) presents another opportunity to either stay in her defining role or take on a different role to further her long-range objectives. With that strategy in mind, she improvises and customizes her reactions depending on what's happening around her. As Mistress Lorelei said, "Becoming a Dominatrix may at first seem schizophrenic, especially if you are still a nice girl. Later you will find the mistress's powers infiltrating your daily life."

When you role-play, you need to be a changeling, a shape-shifter, "switchable" in relation to the particular situation or person. Some bosses and peers may be demanding, others clueless, and still others may need to be taken care of and propped up. Whether you're interacting with a powermonger or someone who needs to be dominated, evaluate each encounter on its own merits—you're going to try on different personas, like you might sample different masks. Allow yourself to experiment, but avoid needlessly spinning your wheels in dead-end situations. Never talked back to a boss? The Amazon might have to make a subtle appearance when called for. Never one to hold back a snarky comment? The Goddess may have to reign you in a bit. Never allowed yourself to be submissive to anyone? The Schoolgirl might have to give you some perspective. Switching archetypes can give you a more holistic outlook and way of being. Before shifting from one role to another, use the Five Ws as a guide to ensure that the "type" you're about to role-play suits the situation:

THE FIVE Ws

The Corporate Dominatrix uses the five Ws as essential tools in the understanding of role-play. Here are things to consider before stepping into character:

- *Who* refers to which role to take to fit the particular situation.
- *Where* refers to given circumstances, surroundings, or context.
- *When* refers to the timing of the action or reaction.
- *What* refers to the issues or potential conflicts at hand.
- *Why* refers to your motives and objectives, as well as those of your colleagues.

As you experiment, the process will eventually become seamless.

"I try to remember to be an Amazon every once in a while, because I always feel like I'm such a Goddess," one client, Amelia, said. "At least now I know what my defining role is, and I can catch myself. I wasn't really conscious that I needed to role-play another archetype sometimes."

Soon you'll learn to do this with ease. A natural Goddess might have to switch to the Governess role if her coworkers are trying to meet a deadline. She'll need to set a schedule, assign tasks, and keep everything moving forward. As the clock is ticking, she's the one cracking the whip! On any given day you may flip between two or three different roles, as if you're looking for the right channel on TV. You have the remote control. In role taking and role-playing, you change persona and your mode of operation to achieve your goal. Every one of us has fantasies that revolve around escaping from our everyday self. Use your imagination to act out, and enjoy yourself! Don't take things so seriously as you experiment, but be careful. You don't want people to get the impression you have multiple personalities or that you've been mixing medications. Subtlety is the key.

ROLE REVERSAL—
DOMINANCE VERSUS SUBMISSION

All of the Corporate Dominatrices exercise some level of dominance; the Schoolgirl is unique, since she borrows her power and is seemingly submissive or imperceptibly dominant. Let's review the six mistress archetypes and their levels of dominance from Chapter Two:

- Highly dominant (Amazon and Queen)
- Moderately dominant (Goddess, Governess, and Nurse)
- Imperceptibly dominant (Schoolgirl)

These labels can help you assess how to bottom from the top, and top from the bottom; reversing roles from dominant to submissive, or submissive to dominant. This is called "role reversal"— perfect for when you're butting heads with another type and need to change strategy.

Belinda, a telecommunications executive, mentioned that her project coordinator had been giving the green light to certain decisions without consulting her. "It's really great when she shows initiative and I know things will be taken care of, but it's not okay when she doesn't at least check in with me at some point." The coordinator was obviously a Queen, but without the same position power as her Queen boss, she needed to be cautious. Belinda needed to give her a WWE smackdown. Administrative Queens are useful because they watch over your domain like it's theirs, but they also need to understand their place in the corporate hierarchy. When you're a subordinate, there's always a time and place to assume the role of the Queen, just don't steamroll over those above you.

Emily became the head of her department after many years of hard work. Even though she was in a dominant position, she was still a Schoolgirl at heart. "I just don't make a lot of hard, big decisions in a vacuum, and I'm okay with my veteran employees suggesting some of them." You can delegate tasks and get input on decisions, but you will begin to lose ground if you're not seen as a formidable leader. As a senior executive, you need to try to regularly activate your Queen to establish yourself.

Kathleen, a Governess assistant to an executive Schoolgirl, was usually in charge of her boss's schedule and even weighed in on decisions that came across her desk. Frustrated with her boss's lack of leadership, she decided to behave differently. "I started deferring to her more, asking her to make decisions about who was in what meeting, asking her to set deadlines on major projects, and asking her to assign accounts. I felt like she needed to start taking charge." Essentially Kathleen was reversing her defining role as the Governess and acting more like a Schoolgirl, so that her boss could grow into a Queen.

REMEMBER THE SCRIPT WHEN YOU TAKE THE STAGE (IMPROVISATION ALLOWED)

As Larry David and his costars do on *Curb Your Enthusiasm*, you can have a rough script, but don't be afraid to ad-lib. Rehearse or practice new roles with trusted friends or colleagues to get comfortable in different situations.

Assuming a role requires you to be mindful of everything:

Your facial expression and body language: What's your look? Are you signaling an emotion you do or don't want to convey? How's your posture, assertive or demure? Does it fit the role you're playing? Try not to slouch in a dominant role or strut in a submissive one.

Your voice: Are you modulating your voice properly? Is it breaking or cracking when you're trying to play a Queen, Nurse, or Amazon role? Your voice should fit the role: firm and direct when delivering a point, or cheerful and bright when playing the Schoolgirl.

Your cues: Are you listening and watching to what others are saying and doing? Pay attention to the nuances, not just the obvious.

Use all of these tips to see how your actions fit into the role you want to portray. Practice your Corporate Dominatrix archetypes by imagining how each one would fit into a particular scene. For example:

The scenario: A company merger has just been announced, and you've got to cope with the new management or move on.

- *Goddess:* There's more to life than work. She sits tight and waits for more information since she doesn't sweat the small stuff.
- *Nurse:* Concerned with the fallout of stress and pressure, she keeps a level head and administers first aid to the emotionally wounded.
- *Governess:* She shifts into organizational hyperdrive, checking to make sure the transitional procedures are in place.
- *Queen:* While trying to increase her influence, she's running a campaign to get face time with the new power brokers to ensure that she comes out in the highest position possible.
- *Schoolgirl:* She's offering to chip in and help with this and that, endearing herself to the new management.
- *Amazon:* Her conquest orientation has her on the lookout for possible turf wars and although she wants to keep the peace, she will go to battle if necessary.

After you've got your acting skills down pat, it is important to see your "performance" in a larger context.

PERCEPTION, MISPERCEPTION, AND REALITY
THROUGH THE C. D. LOOKING GLASS

The trick for women in the workplace is being externally observant and internally resilient. The Corporate Dominatrix knows that success requires 40 percent self-management, 30 percent managing up, and 30 percent managing down. Also remember that corporate life generally revolves around 60 percent executive perception of job performance and commitment, and 40 percent executive reality of job performance and commitment. How many times have you seen colleagues or managers get promotions and raises based on good internal public relations rather than actual execution?

The difference between perception and reality is tricky in S&M—just as it is in business. Perception is, in some cases, more important than reality in the office. Like a funhouse where the mirrors magnify some features rather than others, impressions might not reflect reality. What you think versus what another person thinks of your coworkers, boss, or a particular incident may vary significantly; points of view may be magnified or dwarfed. Fair or not, you've got to be able to read others' perceptions of you because that's what counts in the corporate world.

The reality of the workplace is this: Some people work harder and longer than others and don't get acknowledged for it. Why? All too often, the people who get the credit for being productive and hardworking are those who have a talent for broadcasting this image, even if they don't actually live up to the hype. Are you a workhorse but you keep your head down and your nose clean? You've got to brush up on announcing your contributions to others. Don't assume that a job well done automatically gets noticed—you need to sing your praises loud and clear.

The exercise of taking on different Corporate Dominatrix roles, especially those different from your defining role, can allow you to see other sides of yourself and new possibilities in your career path. This includes checking your baggage outside the building before you enter the office each day. For example, Missy always acted out her defining role, the Amazon, with her boss, and they occasionally butted heads. Missy was never at a loss for opinions, and her supervisor would sometimes be taken aback by her outspokenness in meetings. "I didn't really hold my tongue, even when being more tactful might have helped me get along with him." She was frustrated and felt she was always spinning her wheels.

I asked her if she had felt stymied in the past with other bosses. She said yes, she really did seem to have power issues with people in authority. Acting disruptive and confrontational with her boss wasn't getting her anywhere. No one wants to work with a colleague who wants to face off and always put up a fight. Missy's perception was off—she consistently saw problems in others (i.e., bosses), when it may have been more about her own issues.

The hard truth is that your version of reality within the corporate structure may be skewed because of your own issues. You need to deal with your problems with "the establishment" and work with the people around you. It's counterproductive to always be at odds with your boss or your colleagues—you've got to learn to work with them collaboratively. *Instead of being frustrated by what your supervisor or peers don't know, be energized by what you* do *know and use it to your advantage.*

Everybody's got issues. It's the way of the world. Simple awareness of other people's baggage, as well as your own, and the ability to separate your perceptions from actual reality can help you get ahead. *This takes hypervigilance—watch, listen, and learn.*

If you are proactively aware of your feelings and actions, then that objectivity will help you become a mistress of intuition in the workplace.

CORPORATE MIND GAMES, ADMINISTRATIVE FETISHES, AND EXEC-TRICITIES

Remember the feelings of dread when a lackluster colleague was promoted to be your new supervisor? Or worse, when someone with an awful reputation became your new officemate? Ever work for a control freak know-it-all who constantly looks over your shoulder? Has corporate competition made your coworkers into nauseating sycophants or domineering predators?

What about getting blamed for someone else's mistakes, or having a boss or coworker launch an e-mail blitzkrieg? Has bureaucratic jealousy, envy, or sabotage held you back from a plumb job? Have you ever felt trapped because you hate the job you have but can't afford to quit? Ever received a crappy raise? A less-than-generous bonus? What women fear most is being out of control, bossed or tossed around, and remaining powerless. Given the number of hours we spend at the office and the competition and pressure involved, it's not surprising that emotions sometimes run high, and people behave badly.

Corporate neurotica is commonplace—it's human nature. In fact, it's in the DNA of office life. Be aware that the tug-of-war of the S&M power dynamics can put you into a headlock or power grip if you're not careful. You need to use all of your senses. If you understand the corporate dysfunctionality, you can trump those who exploit it. As I've said before, power is neither good nor bad. It can take you places you want to go, but it can also be a corruptive influence, depending on the way you use it. Recognize the traps for what they are and don't let them trip you up:

HUMILIATION OR EMBARRASSMENT: This dynamic is a favorite of sadists; they feed on others' discomfort, and love to see their peers and subordinates squirm. Don't let yourself fall for it, and don't waste your energy churning with angst. If a colleague or higher-up loves to behave inappropriately, remind them of their manners. Don't accept what doesn't belong to you. (The Governess is the role you would use for this tactic.)

OBJECTIFICATION: Did you ever have a supervisor dismiss you and make you feel insignificant? Have you ever been stared at as if your chest was doing the talking? Don't let yourself get bogged down in identifying with this type of interaction; address it, deal with it, and move on. You will not be ignored. (The Queen is the role you would use for this tactic.)

INFANTALISM AND AGE PLAY: Has your boss talked to you like you were two instead of thirty-two? Being treated like a child is meant to make you feel inferior. Conversely, senior executives can act like babies. Don't fall for it—everyone needs to act their age and you may need to administer a dose of reality. (The Nurse is the role you would use for this tactic.)

EDGE PLAY: Power struggles can put your job, reputation, or even a personal relationship at risk. Is your boss riding you hard or trying to get you to quit? Backstabbing, gossiping, or being overly confrontational are devices used to put you on the defensive. Know when the stakes have been raised and understand what's at risk before you react. Be brave and vigilant. (The Amazon is the role you would use for this situation.)

DEPERSONALIZATION: Are you so caught up in power plays and games that you lose yourself in the process? Make sure throughout all of it, you know who you are and what you stand for—your identity is not something that comes from your career. Remember, you are a valuable human being. (The Goddess is the role you would use for this situation.)

CORPORATE FETISH: Business-related objects that have a magical potency can be BlackBerrys, Treos, cell phones, iPods, and laptops. Obsessively checking voice mail or e-mail can come from a fetishistic drive. The professional landscape runs rampant with gadgets pulling our attention toward our digital fix, and ultimately keeping us tied into work, even after hours. Leaving our desk no longer means leaving our work. We can get e-mails and calls at all hours. I'm all for hard work, but don't allow your gadget fetish to become permanent bondage. You control it; it doesn't control you.

EXEC-TRICITIES: Naughty workplace behavior. How do your colleagues conduct themselves? Do they deviate from the normal, expected, or established routine? Watch your own exec-tricities as well as those of your coworkers—BCCing or CCing the world to watch your back and cover your ass, brown-nosing, grandstanding, intimidation, subversion (withholding important information), level-jumping (going over the supervisor's head), sabotage, and playing follow-the-leader are just some examples. Be alert! Do you have some exec-tricities to add to the mix? I'm sure you've seen everything!

To help you stand up to the various obstacles you'll face in your everyday work life, let's take your personal inventory.

THE CORPORATE DOMINATRIX
SELF-ASSESSMENT

In the list below, place a √ next to those areas that would increase your self-knowledge. Under each item or on a separate sheet of paper, list at least one specific activity you are willing to complete to take more control of your career. I will . . .

___ assume responsibility for my actions and mistakes.

_____

_____

_____

_____

_____

___ identify what bothers me and share what I want and what I need.

_____

_____

_____

_____

_____

___ set limits on what is expected of me.

_____

_____

_____

_____

_____

__ identify communication hot buttons in others. If I don't agree with someone else's response, I let them know in a respectful way.

_____

_____

_____

_____

_____

__ encourage other people to be more forthcoming. I allow them to express their feelings and opinions.

_____

_____

_____

_____

__ learn to say no when necessary.

_____

_____

_____

_____

__ ask for what I want. I don't expect anyone to read my mind or give professional handouts.

_____

_____

_____

_____

NO PAIN, NO GAIN

"The secret of success is learning how to use pain and pleasure instead of having pain and pleasure use you," says Tony Robbins. "If you do that, you're in control of your life. If you don't, life controls you."

Just like working out with weights, working on your personality and coping mechanisms can cause some soreness. We all know that life's challenges can cause discomfort and unpleasantness. But instead of being viewed negatively, the pain should be viewed positively as a stepping-stone to maturity and personal growth; it is just the first step to becoming empowered. Yes, the saying rings true: No pain, no gain. However, if you're spending too much time in pain, you may need to reevaluate where you stand in your job and in your life—role-playing alone will only get you so far.

PLAY IT SAFE

You may recall that the motto of safe, sane, and consensual behavior is a central tenet of S&M. As a good Corporate Dominatrix, you've got to watch the emotional and psychological reactions that might damage others and yourself. Try to stay grounded in what's really happening around you and don't let your mind work overtime. While you should explore the dominant and submissive sides of yourself, the real goal is to establish trust and to have clear, open channels of communication with others.

When things get to be too much, you can turn to the valuable tool of the Corporate Dominatrix—the safe word. This is a word used in S&M practice when the submissive signals that the level of discomfort or pain is too high in a playacted "scene." If a submissive feels the dominant has crossed the line (e.g., a spanking is too severe), she says her safe word and the action is interrupted or ended.

For the Corporate Dominatrix, the safe word is also used to stop a scene; except in this case, it is a scenario that you play over and over again in your head—the "beating" is self-inflicted. For example, if you have an encounter with a colleague, manager, or client, and your response is not your personal best, you may obsessively review that situation in your mind, with thoughts like "I wish I had said this" or "I wish I had done that." We've all been there, but it's important to focus on the future, not the past. The safe word can assist you in doing that.

The safe word helps you resist the impulse or temptation to re-enact conversations or confrontations, and just let it go. In doing so, the scene in your head is interrupted, and you can move past it and learn from it. Choose a safe word that works for you. My friend Marisa just uses the word "stop," while Denise uses "forgiveness."

The safe word is a tool to help you deal with your own doubting internal dialogue. Now let's go over some rules to live by when interacting with others.

THE CORPORATE DOMINATRIX BILL OF MIGHTS

1. The Corporate Dominatrix is fair-minded—she tries to spread that philosophy throughout the company. She isn't out to do harm to others, and she certainly doesn't abuse her power.

2. Trusting your colleagues means trusting your feelings and observations of them.

3. The Corporate Dominatrix cultivates the ability to acquire power and use it wisely.

4. The Corporate Dominatrix overcomes the inherent negative connotations associated with being powerful.

5. The Corporate Dominatrix understands that working with people can be challenging. She helps them be the best they can be, while allowing them be who they have to be. As she grows so do those around her.

6. The Corporate Dominatrix evolves through self-knowledge and a raised consciousness. She knows who she is and what she wants.

7. There is no inbred inequity in the roles of dominant and submissive. Both people are equally deserving of respect and consideration. Everything is done for the benefit of both parties.

8. The exchange of power is truly a balanced exchange. One cannot receive more than one is willing to give.

9. Human beings are capable of an enormous range of emotional feeling, good and bad. Corporate Dominatrices inspire the good and try to control, and possibly heal, the bad.

10. The Corporate Dominatrix continues to seek out mentors while also mentoring others.

Now that you have the Bill of Mights to guide you, let's move on and discover your heart's desire.

FANTASY REALIZATION

There are some people who live in a dream world, and there are some who face reality; and then there are those who turn one into the other.
—Douglas Everett

As a Corporate Dominatrix, you're in the business of making your wildest career dreams come true. The most basic yet possibly the most important process in your transformation is deceptively simple, but it takes work. It rests on one premise: picturing yourself as formidable as well as flexible in your use of all of the archetypes. The first part of fantasy realization involves getting in touch with your inner energy source, but the second half requires you to project that image of power to the world. You can become what you fantasize yourself to be if you make a firm commitment and stick to it.

Interestingly, Gabrielle Oettingen did a study at New York University titled "Expectancy Effects on Behavior Depend on Self-Regulatory Thought." She discovered that "expectations of success guided behavioral commitment towards fantasy realization only when a positive future was mentally contrasted with impeding reality."[14] Her findings support the emergence of goals and the concept of optimism over realism—fantasize it, and it is so. So, why not give fantasy realization a try?

14. Gabriele Oettingen, "Expectancy Effects on Behavior Depend on Self-Regulatory Thought," *Social Cognition* 18, no. 2 (2000): 101.

MANIFEST YOUR DESTINY

What is your professional fantasy? Take a moment and make a list. Do you need the external trappings of power to feel important? Do you want the corner office? Your own staff? Is giving back to the community important to you? Is respect and appreciation critical for job satisfaction? Do you need a certain level of autonomy? Whatever makes you feel relevant and important, no matter how significant or insignificant it may seem, that's okay.

It is *always* helpful to have a five-, ten-, or twenty-year plan in mind. If it makes you more comfortable to think of them as long-term goals, that's fine, too. Fantasy realization is about reclaiming that free feeling you may have had as a child—the feeling that you can use your imagination without pesky limitations. Stay true to yourself—establish a connection so that whatever you envision can be manifested. Here are some steps to consider as you work through the process:

- *Creation:* Use your imagination and desire to *create* your dream job, career, or lifestyle.
- *Selection:* Is the goal that you've set for yourself and your career something that truly suits you? Be sure the dream job you have selected is what you really want.
- *Observation and curiosity:* Have you learned everything you can about your ultimate objective? Try to approach your fantasy with inquisitiveness and devotion.

- *Role modeling:* Choose a role model or multiple role models who embody your fantasy. Look around. Is there anyone who inspires you? How did they get and stay where they are? Keeping these people in mind will help you focus on the qualities you need to become a success.
- *Motivation:* Are you genuinely enthusiastic about reaching your goals? By examining the strength of your inspiration, you will discover just how important the end game is to you.
- *Commitment:* You're not going to get what you want unless you commit on more than one level—short- and long-term dedication is necessary.
- *Entitlement:* Remind yourself that you deserve job satisfaction, and project that with confidence.
- *Expectation:* Feel good about the outcome. Everything happens for a reason.

The above method will help you manifest your fantasy—stay upbeat and be realistic but hopeful about the results. If you have a positive fantasy and a positive reality for attainment, it's more likely to happen. If you have a positive fantasy and a negative reality in which it can materialize, you're going to run into trouble. Giving birth to your fantasy shouldn't be a frustrating or fearful process—it takes hope and confidence. Reawakening to new ideas, a new job, or a new career takes time; rebirth and reinvention doesn't happen overnight. Use that get-up-and-go drive, but remember, success happens at its own pace. Don't delay too long or act too hastily. Let your comfort level guide you as you become the leading lady in your own fantasy.

One reason so few of us achieve what we truly want
is that we never direct our focus; we never concentrate our power.
Most people dabble their way through life,
never deciding to master anything in particular.
—Tony Robbins

DOMMERCISE: Scrapbook Your Way to Success

Scrapbooking is a popular hobby, since most people enjoy recording their memories. Creating a fantasy realization scrapbook looks toward the future—it's where you create a collage or montage of visual and written goals. All you need is a bound notebook or an album that allows for insertion pages—the size of the book depends on your personal preference. Look at it as an arts and crafts project if you like. Break out the art pens, glue, background papers, scissors, and photo covers, and have fun! In addition to collecting and pasting print advertisements, motivational articles, inspirational personality profiles, cartoons, mementos, postcards, and photographs into your book, you can also try journaling. Adding journal or diary entries is therapeutic and provides a great self-exploration exercise. It can also be a problem-solving tool through which you can gain valuable self-knowledge.

Take the opportunity to reflect, and document your innermost thoughts, hopes, and career dreams. Make them tangible and textured with as much detail as you can muster. It might be entertaining to take some personality tests on tickle.com, queendom.com, or yourpersonality.net and include those results for prosperity. This is your professional life unfolding. (*Note:* Through online resources, as well as magazines and books about scrapbooking techniques, explore how others do their scrapbooks. If you are technologically ambitious, you can have a digital scrapbook, too.)

Remember, the fantasy realization scrapbook is a road map for who you want to be, where you are going, and how you plan to get there. Try to dedicate some time once a month to fill a couple of pages. Remind yourself that your vision can come true with hard work and determination. As the Corporate Dominatrix, you can make it happen.

Warning: Don't be fooled into thinking this is child's play. Some of the most powerful personalities on the planet and the savviest businesswomen employ visualization techniques. Jennifer Lopez always knew she would be a star; so did Madonna. Both of these women were consumed with achieving stardom, and they did. You can do it too, if you want it enough.

You can fuel your ambition, activate your fantasy, and realize your dreams because you have the methods of the Corporate Dominatrix (role taking, role-playing, role reversal) and the power necessary to break the chains of command or corporate bondage. You are ready to surpass hurdles that seemed insurmountable before. The necessary ingredient to finding your ultimate career success as the Corporate Dominatrix is the genuine self-confidence and conviction that you will succeed. Without sincere belief in yourself, the six sisters aren't much help, but if you do believe, you can rise to the occasion, and then some. **Good luck, and God bless!**

ACKNOWLEDGMENTS

Part of the Corporate Dominatrix philosophy is giving credit where credit is due, so I would like to thank the Goddesses, Governesses, Queens, Amazons, and Nurses for all their help and support. Patti Adcroft, a Queen if there ever was one, had unshakable faith in me and this project, and without her keen journalistic eye and her not-so-gentle pushing and prodding, I would never have gotten this far. Governesses Kelly Marages, Debra Ginsberg, and Julie Schwartzman provided invaluable input and advice in the early stages of the process. Special thanks to Amy Hughes, a Governess in Schoolgirl clothing, for helping me organize my thoughts and for providing essential structural feedback. Goddesses Claudia Riemer Boutote, Donna Slawsky, Nadine Billard, Andrea Preziotti, and Heidi Krupp were a source of inspiration and creative juice. Nurses Lori Weiss, Lori Ames, and Linda Cunningham gave me positive reinforcement. Thanks to Joelle Delbourgo, my Amazonian agent, for making magic happen.

My publishing experience at Simon Spotlight Entertainment has been wonderful, from my amazingly talented Queen editor,

Tricia Boczkowski, and wildly enthusiastic publisher, Jennifer Bergstrom, to Goddess of Spin Jennifer Robinson and Mistress of Marketing Lucille Rettino. Cara Bedick and Orly Sigal are awesome, and I'm so lucky that these fabulous ladies have my back. Michael Nagin is a Prince among designers—thank you so much for giving *The Corporate Dominatrix* a distinctive visual look and for bringing the Mistress archetypes to life. Katherine Devendorf, Jeannie Ng, Amy Wilson, Tom Finnegan, and Dorothy Gribbin worked behind the scenes to keep me focused, honest, and on track with the publishing schedule. Thanks to Kai Falkenberg for the legal green light, and muchas gracias to SJ for always being there. Abrazos and besos to Joey P. and Sylvia for the imaginative photo shoot.

M. Louise Ripley is an academic Goddess and I so appreciate her making the time to provide a foreword to *The Corporate Dominatrix*. Special thanks to Lorelei, author of *The Mistress Manual*.

Finally, I'm very blessed to have a marvelous husband and outstanding parents—thank you for being my cheerleading squad.